Reading, Writing, and the Study of Literature

Arthur W. Biddle
Toby Fulwiler

University of Vermont

Random House New York

Library of Congress Cataloging-in-Publication Data

Biddle, Arthur W.   Reading, writing, and the study of literature.

Includes bibliographies and index.   1. English language—Rhetoric.   2. Criticism—Authorship.   3. Report writing.   I. Fulwiler, Toby, 1942–   .   II. Title.
PE1479.C7B54   1989   808'.0668   88-18279 ISBN 0-394-37404-5

Cover Photo Research: Giraudon/Art Resource, N.Y. Bonnard, *The Window.*
Cover and Text Design: Sandra Josephson

Manufactured in the United States of America

Acknowledgments

"The Follies of Writer Worship" by Julian Barnes. Copyright 1985 by Julian Barnes; Copyright 1930, 1939 by Holt, Rinehart and Winston, Inc.

"The Death of the Hired Hand" by Robert Frost. Copyright 1958 by Robert Frost. Copyright 1967 by Lesley Frost Ballantine. Reprinted from *The Poetry of Robert Frost* edited by Edward Connery Lathem, by permission of Henry Holt and Company, Inc.

Airships by Barry Hannah. Copyright 1978 by Barry Hannah. Reprinted by permission of Alfred A. Knopf, Inc.

"Coda" by David Huddle. Copyright 1988 by David Huddle, from *Stopping by Home.*

"The Red Wheelbarrow" by William Carlos Williams. *Collected Poems, Volume I: 1909–1939.* Copyright 1938 by New Directions Publishing Corporation.

Preface

We wrote *Reading, Writing, and the Study of Literature* to introduce you to those approaches that are basic to the serious study of literature. Students taking their first college course in literature will find this book worthwhile. English majors and minors will find it essential.

The field of English is broad and diverse, encompassing the history, interpretation, and appreciation of the best writing in the English-speaking world. But the study of English also includes the writing we do ourselves and our attempts to improve it, as we learn to revise, edit, and craft our own language into meaningful wholes. Therefore, this book approaches literary study from two distinct yet interlocking perspectives. First, we look at the major genres of literature—fiction, poetry, and drama. In chapters written by experts in each field, we examine the aspects of those genres you need to know to join the continuing dialogue about how each works. Second, we examine what might be called "student genres," those forms in which students of literature are expected to express their ideas about the literature they read.

Reading, Writing, and the Study of Literature addresses the conventions of literary study from the viewpoint of one who not only reads literature, but also writes about it. In the Prelude we treat the relationships between reading and writing as they pertain to literary study, focusing first on reading as a writer and then on writing as a reader. We believe that the more students write about literature, the better they will understand it; and conversely, the more literature they read, the better they will write.

The Design of This Book

Part I—Reading as a Writer—considers literature primarily from the point of view of the reader, providing perspectives on the genres into which literature is commonly divided—fiction, poetry, and drama. This section begins with Toby Fulwiler's chapter "Journal Writing," which suggests ways in which informal writing about novels, poems, and plays creates both engagement and understanding on the part of readers. The next three chapters focus on the genres themselves. The writers of these chapters make no attempt to offer the last word on each genre—such an aim is clearly outside the scope of this book. Instead, the authors describe their own particular experiences with fiction, poetry, or drama.

In Chapter 2, "Responding to Fiction," Arthur W. Biddle and Allen Shepherd look at fiction primarily as storytelling. At the same time, they point out those features of novels and short stories which make them special.

In Chapter 3, "Responding to Poetry," Sidney Poger treats poetry as the genre which most deliberately plays with language. The chapter begins, however, with a close look at the generation of a single poem, examining the changes in word choices from draft to draft that lead eventually to the finished poem.

In Chapter 4, "Responding to Drama," James Howe asks us to "read" drama in terms of performance. His essay explores those qualities that set drama apart from the other literary genres, as well as some of the features it shares with film and television.

In this section's final chapter, "Literary Criticism and Theory," James Holstun provides an overview of current critical theories, theories about the nature of literature and how best to study it. Those new to serious literary study will find this chapter invaluable.

Part II of this book—Writing as a Reader—focuses on the forms of writing students are commonly expected to master as they study literature in college. Each chapter in this section examines closely one of what might be called "the student genres," those forms in which students are expected to express their knowledge and ideas about literature.

In Chapter 6, "Writing Critical Essays," Robyn Warhol describes the assumptions and expectations behind the assignment most commonly associated with college English classes. She analyzes three types of critical essays and suggests practical approaches for writing each.

In Chapter 7, "Writing Personal Essays," Mary Jane Dickerson suggests an unusual kind of response to reading literature. She includes a useful checklist of questions student writers might ask themselves as they write in this mode.

In Chapter 8, "Imaginative Writing and Risk Taking," William Stephany presents a variety of unorthodox but creative approaches to writing about literature. He shows some of the possibilities for this kind of writing, including parody and imitation, and also gives practical advice to the writer.

In Chapter 9, "Writing Essay Examinations," Anthony Magistrale takes the reader step-by-step through strategies that lead to writing successful essays about literature in the pressure-packed environment of one- and two-hour sit-down examinations.

In Chapter 10, "Writing Research," Richard Sweterlitsch offers a rationale for college-level literary research. Included in this chapter is helpful advice on interviewing and site visits, as well as library work. The latest MLA documentation format is explained.

How To Read This Book

We believe this book works well when read straight through. The reader must reflect on the differences and similarities of both the "literary genres" and the "student genres," discovering in one text an introduction to the multifaceted and rapidly changing field of English studies.

However, we also believe the book can profitably be read in bits and pieces, by mixing and matching sections from Parts One and Two as needed. In fact, we conceived the book with this method of use in mind. Thus, the student who needs to write a critical essay about poetry would focus on Chapters 6 and 3. Another student preparing for essay exams in a novel course might study Chapters 9 and 2. Someone beginning a survey course might read Chapter 1, "Journal Writing," followed by appropriate chapters on the literary genres as required by the course reading assignments, then read chapters on student genres as required by the writing assignments.

We do recommend that all students read the first two essays in this book. The Prelude introduces the whole work by exploring the nature of the reading/writing relationship in the study of literature. Chapter 1, "Journal Writing," demonstrates our belief that most students would profit from recording and documenting their reading experiences in a journal.

Acknowledgments

The authors wish to thank the many people who helped us write this book. Heading the list are our students, especially A. De Battiste, who read and responded to drafts of many chapters and contributed the writing samples you'll find throughout. Colleagues assisted too, especially Ghita Orth and Huck Gutman, University of Vermont. The authors are also grateful for the suggestions made by Robert DiYanni, Pace University; C. William Griffin, Virginia Commonwealth University; and Tom Waldrep, University of South Carolina. Thank you all.

Burlington, Vermont

Arthur W. Biddle
Toby Fulwiler

CONTENTS

Contents

Contents

Contents

PRELUDE

Reading and Writing in College

Arthur W. Biddle
and Toby Fulwiler

☐

When I was young, reading and writing were great because I felt like a big person. As I grew older, I realized that all this fun was getting harder.

Krista, first-year college student

If you like to read and write, find these activities easy, and do them well, you'll have a good time in college literature classes. As Chris, a sophomore in one of our classes, wrote in his journal: "When I'm in the right mood, and have the right book, it goes down like cream. In 11th grade, my English teacher told us to pretend to be the characters in the book. I made it through one of Russell Baker's stories being a paper boy." However, for many students, not all reading "goes down like cream." Bill, a freshman, explained his attitude this way: "I've never liked reading, especially textbook reading. I don't think I've ever read a book for pleasure except when I was younger. . . . If I read a book I like, I don't mind reading at all, but I guess that's kind of silly because nobody likes to read a book he doesn't like." Meanwhile, Julie, another sophomore, told us: "As far back as I can remember, I have always preferred reading to writing. I think it's because I always found reading easy—I could always sit down and just read for hours (if a book was interesting) without even being told."

1

When we asked students in this same class about writing, we found mixed opinions as well. Hollis, a junior, told us what many of our students said: "I like to write, but it's very difficult for me unless I like what I am writing about." Peter, a freshman, said he enjoyed writing except in the "college application mode. You know, 'What was your most rewarding nonacademic activity?' or 'Write an essay telling us something about yourself.' That's the kind of writing I can't deal with." Students usually like to write about subjects they choose and in forms with which they are familiar. No surprises here.

In other words, if you are like some of our students, you bring with you mixed emotions toward reading and writing about various kinds of literature. While most of you have positive experiences reading and writing in private, many of you have some negative experiences when one or the other is assigned in school. In the rest of this essay, we'd like to look more closely first at reading and then at writing, and see if we can't make a sort of peace between our private needs as readers and writers and the more public demands of the academic community.

□

The Way You're Supposed to Read

The way you're *supposed* to read fiction, poetry, and drama in order to comprehend them fully—as you need to do in order to write essays and examinations about them or discuss them in class—goes something like this: You sit at your desk, text in front of you, notebook open, pen poised. As you read, you mark important passages in the text; you summarize main ideas and trace recurrent themes in your notebook. You look up in a dictionary, encyclopedia, or glossary all words, names, ideas you do not understand. And if you are reading a novel or poem or a play, you pay particular attention to certain technical elements of the text.

Susan, a seasoned student of literary study, describes the *shoulds* of fiction reading this way: "I have learned that there are a lot of things to look for when I read. For example, who is narrating? Does the narrator change? What is the author's style? What is the point of view from which the story is told? When I read, however, I don't always like to look for these things. I just like to read for the sake of reading. I don't like to read into stories as much as my former professors have done." While Susan clearly knows *how* she's supposed to read and *what* she's supposed to look for, a part of her rebels and wants to read more intuitively or impressionistically, with less deliberately analytical attention than some of her teachers have insisted on.

College students are not alone in rebelling against the kind of academic toughness that good reading is supposed to entail. In fact, one of the contributing authors in this volume confessed in his journal:

When I read strictly for myself, late at night in bed or through sunglasses on the beach, I violate most of the rules I learned about how to read well. When an image or incident triggers a memory, I let myself daydream and wander off with it. When I don't know what a word means, I skip it. When I find the plot slow moving, I skim until things pick up again. When I'm not in the mood for one book, I start another, and again another. Right now I'm reading about 7 books, 3 magazines, and a couple of catalogues. I no longer consider it a moral obligation to start a book at the beginning, to avoid peeking at the end, or to finish it once started.

To remember something that strikes me as especially interesting, I write a note in the margin, dog-ear a page, or sometimes read the passage out loud to my wife. But I seldom trace plot, character, theme, or symbol methodically from page to page, beginning to end. Often I am confident that I understand the meaning of what I've read—but am not always sure that I could write a coherent essay about it.

Don't misunderstand—we're not making fun of either approach to reading, the rigorously academic or the casually private. It is not our purpose in this book to give you either negative lessons or simplistic formulas about reading literature. We think that serious reading in the academic community is, in many important ways, quite compatible with private enjoyment—but some adjustments may be useful. Reading itself is a complex intellectual activity, governed by conventions and not reducible to foolproof rules. We read, in other words, as members of one or several communities with certain assumptions and expectations that inevitably influence our reading. We do this—consciously or unconsciously—whether we read on the beach or in the classroom.

□

Reading to Understand

The authors of this book no longer believe that we, or anybody else for that matter, will ever perfectly understand the central meaning of the stories, poems, or plays we read, no matter how well we prepare ourselves. Each reader brings to any reading a background unique socially, economically, religiously, politically, esthetically, and intellectually. In other words, our personal history, even our present mood, influences our responses, and so makes each reading to some significant extent our own.

A few simple examples will show what we mean. Last semester, when one of our classes read John Steinbeck's novel about dispossessed farmers, *The Grapes of Wrath,* one student saw reflected in the plight of Steinbeck's

Okies her own family's difficulties holding onto their Vermont dairy farm. Another student, a practicing Christian, found meaning in the parallels and dissonances between the lives of several characters and the biblical accounts of Jesus's life. Which reading was "correct"? Both? Neither? An obviously unfair question. As these readers were responding to the words of *The Grapes of Wrath,* they were collaborating with Steinbeck in the creation of a text. We believe that in a very real sense any text is created anew—written if you like—by the reader.

Not only does each reader bring something different to a work, but each rereading is different. The second time around, we build on that initial reading, noticing things that escaped us earlier, seeing indications of what is to come, finding patterns impossible to discern the first time. Too, we have become different readers than we were before, and if months or years have passed, we may have changed so significantly that the work itself no longer is the same. In fact, when we reread, we usually find it easier to follow the rules of good reading because we know so much better what the work is about.

It is not restating the obvious to suggest that we read anything better when it is already familiar to us. Consequently, we cannot make sense of any text—literary, scientific, or otherwise—if we don't already know what most of the words, concepts, and formulas mean. Any literature is approachable only because it builds on what we already know. We can understand older characters such as Falstaff, Lady Macbeth, and King Lear because they have traits we have seen in people we already know. We understand younger characters such as Oliver Twist, Holden Caulfield, and Caddy Compson because we have felt some of what they feel. The trick for an author is to give us enough of what we already understand in order to lead us where we have no firsthand knowledge—be it medieval England, Victorian London, Pencey Prep, or a shabby household in Mississippi.

So, in a very real sense, when we read a poem, play, or short story, a part of what we read we already know. From that vantage of familiarity we view the rest, the unknown. Ideally, we can engage the piece on a personal, as well as an academic, level and so make it *our own.* If we cannot do this, cannot identify with the narrator, or some character or character trait, or some aspect of the situation, we may have difficulty enjoying the work or understanding it well enough to profit from it.

□

Reading as a Writer

Everyone who reads this book is a writer. Everyone who wrote this book is a reader. Of course. We have found that when you *read as a writer,* your relationship to the text changes. What do we mean *read as a writer?* Well, first, understand that you, we, and people like Flannery O'Connor don't come from three different planets. We all struggle to get control of an idea, to find the words that belong to that idea, and then to present that idea in those words intelligibly and, we hope, with a little grace. Those stories, poems, and plays in magazines and textbooks were written by human beings just like us. You've probably written a story or two, maybe some poetry, certainly a lot of papers. So have we. Realizing that published words were written by men and women pretty much like yourself may not be a great revelation, but it can change the way you read, the attention you pay to words and works, and, in turn, the way you actually write. Here's what we mean:

Humanity.   The visitor to William Faulkner's home in Oxford, Mississippi, will find on the desk in his study a clear sign of the great writer's humanity—a blue and white plastic Vick's inhaler. The author of "Barn Burning" and *The Sound and the Fury* sometimes suffered from nasal congestion! To read as a writer, it helps to know that even the greatest authors are mortal—that they catch cold and that they were once students and apprentices as we are now.

Comparing notes, the authors of this volume find themselves well aware of their own failings and imperfections as writers. We know too well that nothing we write is ever perfect—yet we do write books and articles and get them published. So too, we reason, must the great writers often feel about the limits of their own powers. And this realization—like the Vick's inhaler—helps reduce those giants to human size. If you've ever seen an author's early manuscript drafts, you know of the professional's willingness to revise and edit. As a student of literature, eventually you come to understand that any text is a "made" object, that it didn't spring full-blown from the mind of God or the muse of poetry. There was never any inevitability about it. It was probably sweated over, rewritten, and discussed just as your best writing is, and the printed version we study may be the third or the thirtieth rewrite.

Questions.   As writers ourselves, we've become aware that almost all written works originate as responses to certain questions or problems. Behind virtually everything we write is a question: Behind a shopping list is the question "What do we need at the store?" Behind a letter home is the question "How are you? or "How am I?" Behind a laboratory report is the question "What happened?" Sometimes, of course, the piece of writing doesn't answer the question well, or tries to answer a group of questions all at once, or asks still more questions. However, looked at this way, most pieces of writing make more sense and seem more approachable and understandable.

5

Answers.   When we write something ourselves, we struggle to answer a question or solve a problem. Of course, it doesn't always work out the way we intend. But watching ourselves work helps us to understand the efforts of other writers. We've also learned where many of those structured answers come from—the writing itself. We've come to realize that the very act of composing is an answer-creating, problem-solving activity. Writers often discover their answers in the process of writing. More than one novelist has told about characters "taking over" and creating a new direction for the second half of a book.

How does this help you as a reader? It lets you know that if you want to figure out a particularly puzzling part of what you're reading, you too should write and see what solutions you discover. As readers, we are still writers. We can use writing to solve reading problems. Our experience as writers also tells us that there is usually more than one answer to any given question. The story that ends one way might have ended differently had the author been in another mood, place, or time. The modern sonnet might have been done in free verse. Hamlet might have survived Act V. Realizing this, the reader-as-writer knows that the author has made choices, that these choices produce certain effects, and that other choices might have been made and would have produced different effects.

Seeing Words.   The writer's struggle to write is frequently a struggle to find the right words. Sometimes they come, and just as often they don't. Consider the genius of those who bat better than .500. As a writer, you can appreciate the way a word just fits, seems to be the only word that will do. Sometimes when you recognize one of these words on the page, you get the feeling that you know how pleased the author must have been to find it. Walt Whitman's description of the live oak "solitary in a wide flat space, *uttering* joyous leaves all its life" and Emily Dickinson's "certain *slant* of light, winter afternoons" induce a little shiver of rightness. You'll have your own favorites, of course. When you read with an awareness of how you and other writers select words, you'll understand better the writer's craft.

Hearing Rhythms.   In our own struggle to construct sentences and paragraphs that sound fluid to the ear, we appreciate better the same struggle in the writers we read. We notice constructions that work, that have a particular balance, that are deliberately parallel (as we are making this one), that see long sentences set off by short ones. As writers ourselves, we marvel at the apparent ease with which a Henry James or a Toni Morrison pulls these off. Of course, we never know for sure whether they rolled easily off the author's pen or whether he or she struggled as we so often do.

Tracing Themes.   In our own writing, we search for just the right pattern or repetition or other signal to keep readers clearly on the track. We may

6

rearrange sections to make this happen and feel good when it works out, especially in longer pieces in which holding parts together is especially difficult. Then when we become readers, we look harder to see how other authors accomplish the same thing. Sometimes, of course, the search is made more difficult because the theme is subtly embedded in the text, as it is in a James Joyce short story, for instance, where little seems to happen. So we learn to reread such texts to discover what else is there.

Understanding Metaphor and Symbol.   If you've ever tried to use figurative language to express your meaning, you probably stand in awe of the great masters of imaginative literature. The judicious but occasionally outrageous use of metaphor and symbol is often what sets the great writers apart: Ezra Pound's likening of faces in a subway crowd to "petals on a wet, black bough;" Wordsworth's image of "life's star," the soul, "trailing clouds of glory."

Sometimes, too, great metaphors become great symbols, like Keats's "Grecian Urn," Thoreau's "Walden Pond," Melville's "Moby Dick," or Plath's "Bell Jar." As a writer reading, you can watch how any particular effect is created. Think of alternatives. Look for continuity and extension—how long can she get away with that? Where will she bring it in again? Of course, literary critics train themselves to look for these features. But when you come at the problem of creating workable metaphor and symbol as a writer yourself, you read with more empathy and understanding.

Noticing Starts, Stops, Transitions, and Conventions.   The writer as reader is far more likely to notice how other writers handle even the elementary problems of composition. If you always have trouble with first lines in whatever you write, you're more likely to notice how published authors start their pieces. You may read with awe a line like "Call me Ishmael," and at other times wonder, "Why did he start there?" You dig deeper into the work and begin to second-guess the author. You might notice how a key word at the end of one paragraph prepares you for what is coming in the next (or deliberately does not). You see this because you too work hard at transitions. And even the smaller matters, such as how white space allows the writer a sharp break in continuity, how semicolons function in certain situations, how good titles set up reader expectations (or the effects of sentence fragments such as this one). Readers who are also writers observe these and many other composition tricks because they are thinking about how they too might use them in their own writing.

Rereading and Rewriting.   We've discovered that when writing something fairly long and complicated, we need to reread our work to know where it has been and where it needs to go next. If we have that problem *as writers,* is it any wonder that we also have it as readers? Many lengthy and complex works need more than one reading to make complete sense. The first time through is full of surprises—turns of plot, quirks of character, rediscovered memories and associations. In other words, we're so busy *having* the reading experience that there is little opportunity to reflect on or interpret that experience. It is understandable that the first time through a novel, play, or poem we have difficulty seeing close internal relationships and structural and symbolic subtleties. So, we plan on rereading the great texts as carefully and curiously as we do our own.

□

Writing as a Reader

The same kinds of *shoulds* surround writing as reading. That is, many students have come to believe that writing privately is one thing, but writing for an academic public quite something else. Melissa, a sophomore, describes it this way in her journal: "Writing, Writing, Writing! Umm, I love it, but I'm told that I'm not allowed to use the verb "to be." I've also been told to never use "never" and never use "always"! Write with description. Action verbs are best." Writing for an academic audience *is,* of course, different from writing for oneself, but maybe not quite in the way Melissa describes.

In the last section we discussed the concept of reading as a writer. In this section, we'd like to explore the other side of that coin, "writing as a reader." We write as readers in at least three distinct ways: First, when we learn how and in what contexts and with what struggles the great works were created, we also learn about our own writing. Second, we need to remember that much of what we write is directed ultimately at other readers whose needs we must anticipate. Third, we write to please ourselves, using all the techniques at our disposal to help generate prose and poetry that satisfies our own sense of rightness. Let's look at each of these perspectives in turn.

Lessons from the Masters

One of the problems with literary study is the distance we often feel between those who write the great works of literature and the rest of us who write *about* them. That's why it can be helpful to remember that the great writers themselves were once students of other great writers, and that they too worked hard on their writing to get it just right. When you read the finished works of Jane Austen or Henry David Thoreau or T. S. Eliot, keep in mind that these writers filled notebook after notebook with observations and ideas that only later, and sometimes after many drafts, bore fruit as the finished works we so celebrate today. Keep in mind also that

8

many published authors had mentors—friends, spouses, teachers, editors—who helped them clarify and refine their ideas, images, characters.

Learning to write well—and continuing to do so—is often a messy, frustrating business. Once you've mastered the conventions and forms of written composition, you need to remember that each time you set out to write something new—a critical essay, a personal narrative, a research proposal, or a poem—each time you need to start all over to develop and order your ideas, always asking "have I said this as clearly, concisely, believably, or gracefully, as possible?"

Most of us who have learned to write with some competence consider writing a fairly unpredictable, multistage process, in which we need to find and capture ideas in the first place, develop them in some reasonably clear sequence according to some reasonably clear logic, support them with good examples remembered or researched, and make sure the whole composition is written in a style appropriate to the audience and purpose. Along the way, many of us have learned to rely on the same tricks that helped Austen, Thoreau, and Eliot: to record our insights and observations informally in notebooks or journals; to begin writing before we have fully developed our ideas, trusting that the act of writing itself will help work them out; to plan to write more than one draft of anything important; to receive a little help from our friends; and to edit ceaselessly to get the final product just right. We've also learned that there are few guarantees in the act of writing: Sometimes ideas that seemed brilliant in the shower or on the jogging path look pale on paper; at other times, ideas that start out routinely develop into something quite original and pleasing.

So it may help you, as it helps us, occasionally to remember that writing well wasn't necessarily any easier for the masters than it is for us and that the techniques that helped them may help us as well.

Writing for Other Readers

When we write for other readers, we need to write with care, with courtesy, and with doubt. We write carefully that they may follow the thread of our thought and not be thrown off by distractions. We write courteously out of respect for our readers and in order to be taken seriously. And we write with doubt, anticipating that our readers will be curious and ask questions. We'll look briefly at some of the techniques writers use when they think carefully about their readers.

Conventions.   Writers who use the standard conventions of written English treat their readers with respect and care. At the same time, they usually guarantee a fair hearing for whatever they have to say. To misuse the conventions, whether punctuation, spelling, grammar, or format, is to violate your readers' expectations and therefore to distract them. This is not to say that the violation of expectations has no place in writing, for we know it does. Just keep in mind that when it's done by a Walt Whitman, a Virginia Woolf, or an e. e. cummings, it's done deliberately and with purpose. So, know what you're doing.

Information and Explanation.   In writing notes to ourselves, we often use shorthand and abbreviations because we fill in the rest from our heads. But as soon as we begin writing to others, we start asking: How much do my readers already know? What else will they need in order to understand me? Many college students writing to academic audiences don't know how much to assume of their readers. If you are not sure, we recommend that you err by providing too much information rather than too little: When you mention literary works, at least the first time, give full titles, authors, dates. When you use literary terminology or concepts (like *point of view, existentialism,* or *pastoral*), either define them or make sure your examples do that for you.

Evidence.   As you write, try to consider the kind of evidence *you* require in order to believe someone or be persuaded to accept their perspective. As a reader yourself, you may find that you are seldom convinced by vague generalities or unsupported assertions—at least we seldom are. This means that when you write personal narrative, remember to create belief by supplying concrete detail of character and situation from remembered experience. When you write critical essays, give specific evidence from texts or documented support from experts. And when you write imaginatively, support your imaginings with details and facts—or the illusion of details and facts.

Language and Style.   The language in which we write makes it easy for our readers to understand us, or it doesn't. It demonstrates our understanding of our subject, or our ignorance. When we write letters to friends, we use a fairly informal talky style. When we write term papers for a Shakespeare professor, we adopt a more formal, analytical style. (And when we write books for college students, we try to fall somewhere in between.) In thinking about who is going to read our writing (our audience), we adjust word choice, sentence structure, perhaps even punctuation and paragraphing to match our intentions with their expectations.

Transitions.   The more we become attuned to the needs of our audience, the more important become the little words that connect one sentence to another by showing the relationship between ideas—words like *so, thus, then, however, meanwhile, nevertheless, and, but, first, next, last, on the one hand, in other words, in addition, finally.* These words do not always show up the first time we write a draft, when we're worried more about getting the basic ideas down. But as we rework drafts to make our text as clear as possible, we add signals and cues like these to point readers—as unmistakably as we can—in the right direction.

Documentation.   Documentation is another reader courtesy, necessary whenever the writer uses the words, data, or ideas of another. Through in-text references or footnotes, we tell where to find all the assertions and expert opinions used to support our arguments. We explain who said what, where, and when. Readers who are curious can trace these references and find out still more. The *MLA Handbook for Writers of Research Papers* (third edition) contains explanations of how to document your work in literature classes.

Titles and Headings.   We're amazed at how often novice writers ignore some of their most powerful tools—titles and headings. A good title (both descriptive and provocative, if possible) not only announces your subject, but creates a favorable attitude toward your piece. Section headings (like those you see in this chapter) guide your reader through an essay. We find that creating subheads *as we write* helps us understand where we are in our writing task, tells us where to go next, and even gives us a marked block of text to relocate elsewhere if revision demands it.

Writing for Ourselves

Our first audience is always ourselves. Remember this, especially when you're blocked or confused or uncertain of exactly what you want to say. At such times, it can actually be a hindrance to worry about your audience. Instead, you must ask yourself: Where do *I* want to go? What is the point *I* want to make in the first place? Do *I* understand where my text leads so far? Where does it need to go next?

While we have been describing writing that is primarily academic, we think the same suggestions hold true for imaginative writing—maybe even more so. Before a fiction writer can worry too much about "reader cues," she or he needs to be pretty certain that his or her "writer cues" are in order; in other words, the writer needs to see *for himself or herself* that the character development is consistent, the setting true to imagination or memory, the plot one the writer believes in. Before a poet can think about potential reader responses to images, rhymes, or rhythms, he or she first has to see them in his or her own eye, hear them with his or her own ear to test their ring of truth. As writers, we are readers, first and last—readers of our own language, whether it be directed through letters to family and friends, through essays to teachers, or through journals, intended from the outset to stay quite close to ourselves.

PART ONE

□

Reading as a Writer

□

CHAPTER 1

Journal Writing

Toby Fulwiler

□

For me the journal is not simply a place to record my thoughts, but a place to develop them more objectively; it acts as sort of a mirror for my ideas.

When we write about anything, we learn it better. In fact, I think the most important reason to write in the first place is for ourselves, for what happens in our own minds when we make concrete our otherwise scattered and fragmentary thought. Finding words, generating sentences, constructing paragraphs is also our way of finding, generating, and constructing the meaning of our world. In other words, one of the most powerful reasons for writing is not to convey a message *to* someone else, but to find out for ourselves that we have a message and that we understand its shape and content.

This is where journals come in: they are notebooks kept by writers and thinkers primarily for themselves as a means of methodically locating, collecting, and making sense of their own thoughts. When we write to ourselves, as we do in journals, diaries, and notebooks, we concentrate on what *we* are thinking about, rather than the shape of our words or how some distant audience will react to them.

□

Assigned Journals

Journals written for college classes differ from private diaries written for yourself. While historically the two terms have been used interchangeably, today we can make a useful distinction between them: diaries are personal notebooks that contain private thoughts, memories, feelings, dreams—things of importance to the writer and nobody else. Journals, however, have a more limited focus; they center more on the point where writers' personal lives meet their intellectual and social lives—in this case, centering on that meeting as it takes place in the study of literature.

If your English teacher has asked you to keep a journal, it is probably with the hope that you will use it to locate, collect, and make sense of your thoughts about the content of your literature class: about your reactions to the novels, plays, or poems; about your role in class discussions; about your candid reactions to particular lectures; about first ideas for writing assignments and later thoughts on revising those assignments; about connections between this course and others you are taking. And about the personal connections you may make between this course and the rest of your life—whatever they may be.

It might also help to separate journals from class notebooks. Unlike diaries, class notebooks contain almost nothing at all that is personal, being filled as they are with other people's ideas: lecture and discussion notes, copied quotations, next week's assignments, and so on. These notebooks are especially useful to help you pass examinations, but that's about it. Think of your journal as a cross between a diary (subjective) and a class notebook (objective): in the journal you write about the object of study from your own personal perspective—and you write primarily to yourself. Here's how I might diagram that difference:

DIARY - - - - - - - - JOURNAL - - - - - - - - CLASS NOTEBOOK

The key difference between a diary kept exclusively for yourself and a journal assigned for a class is obvious: your professor will probably want to look at your journal from time to time. She or he may want to look through it to see what you are thinking about William Shakespeare, Herman Melville, or Nikki Giovanni. If your teacher wants to look at your journal, chances are good that it is not to grade it in any conventional sense. More likely, the teacher wants to see if you have written regularly, often, and at length, about ideas related to the course. I cannot, of course, guarantee that your teacher will look at it this way. That is simply how most English teachers I know use journals. You'll have to check with your teacher to be sure.

Students commonly have questions about journals; they wonder about the mix of public and private expected in an assigned journal. In fact, one student, Missy, described her concern this way:

> 9/3 For three years now I've kept a journal on my own—a personal one, that I sort of talk to when I'm troubled or confused about things. It's like talking to a friend who just listens with great patience and never argues with me. But now I'm supposed to keep one for my English class and I'm not sure how that will work—I don't see how I can write personal things in a book that my professor is going to read. How can a journal be both personal and kept for a class at the same time?

Good questions. In the rest of this chapter, I will try to lay out the territory of the journal to make clear what it might look like, how it might work, and what you might put in it.

□

Unassigned Journals

It is entirely possible that your literature instructor has not asked you to keep a journal—or has made it a recommendation and intends to do nothing specifically or formally with it. In either case, the journal is one assignment you may choose to do yourself, independent of any instructional intention. Few of us would write other academic assignments on our own—term papers, for instance—without being required to. But many people do elect to keep journals because they are both intellectually useful and easy to do.

As a literature student, you will find that personal notebooks (sometimes called journals and sometimes diaries) have a long and respected literary history. Some authors even became famous because they wrote private accounts of their lives: Samuel Pepys's *Diary* remains one of the liveliest accounts of seventeenth-century England in existence; James Boswell's eighteenth-century *London Journal* is as famous as anything else he wrote. Many of us know Anaïs Nin only because of the *Diaries* in which she describes life in mid-twentieth-century Paris. Some journals, such as those by William Byrd and William Bradford in the seventeenth century, are especially useful for their historical information about the settlement of colonial America—as were the nineteenth-century journals of the explorers Lewis and Clark.

As a teacher of nineteenth-century American literature, I can attest to the centrality of journals to the lives of some of our best writers. Those of Ralph Waldo Emerson and Henry David Thoreau contain nearly all the germinal ideas and language for their later well-known masterpieces. *Walden,* in fact, retains many of the characteristics of an actual journal; it takes readers chronologically through the cycle of a year, from summer to spring. Journals, diaries, and letters are also interesting because they provide crucial insights into the personalities of complex writers.

Journals are worth your while for another reason: they really do help you sort out your ideas while you are taking the course. They help you understand what your are reading, which in turn helps you participate with more confidence in class discussion. They help you prepare for exams, because whenever you write about an idea, you improve your chances of remembering it. And they help if you have formal papers to write, because they let you try out and play with ideas before you commit them to the judgment to which essays and term papers are usually subjected.

Then too, journals prove to be documents worth saving and rereading at other times in your life. Sometimes the real value of a journal isn't even apparent until months or years later, when the writer or the writer's family finds it a remarkable record of thought frozen in time, revealing as do photograph albums a person at another stage of development. Every time I reread an old journal of mine I find it a benchmark against which to measure my current life. Having kept journals on and off since I was a college sophomore, I have lots of benchmarks.

For some time now, I have asked students in my American literature classes to keep journals to help them understand the books, authors, ideas, and environment that constitutes literary study. In general, I have found the journals to be the best writing assignment I give: the frequent writing both in class and out allows all of us time to find and share insights. My students seem to like the noncompetitive climate journals encourage; I enjoy the way journals let me see my students' more candid reactions to the books they read in the course.

In the rest of this chapter, I will share with you some of the uses my students have found for journals in their study of American literature. I trust that students of any literary period or genre may find good ideas here.

□

Writing About Reading

One specific way to use your journal is to write about everything you read. Keep your journal with your books, and every time you read a chapter or an article, jot down your reaction to what you just read. Don't worry about sounding profound; try instead to pin down and express what interests or annoys you or makes your curious or confused. Write honestly in your own voice. If you have a little more time, reflect on why you reacted as you did—why were you excited, angry, bored, empathetic, sympathetic? In the following entry, David writes about his first encounter with Herman Melville's long novel *Moby Dick:*

> Moby has begun. It's nice to be reading a story again in-
> stead of the transcendentalists. . . . I actually had a
> lot of fun with Ralph, Hank, and Walt, but I'm ready for
> a novel. Herman says some cool things right from the
> start. He is fascinated with water. . . .

I hear the voice of the David I know in class—a bright and good-humored sophomore. In this entry he writes as he talks, easily and with a slight irreverence, yet showing he's read the work and is ready to talk about it in his own terms.

In the process of reading, it's always a good idea to guess and conjecture about what's going on, because that helps you keep track of what you read, as well as read with more focus. In the following entry, also about *Moby Dick,* Susan expresses her apprehensions about how the novel will end:

> It's an awful thing to say, but I wish Starbuck had
> killed Ahab with that musket. If Ahab is shot there will
> be only one life lost, but since Starbuck decides not to
> do it, I have a feeling the whole crew will be lost be-
> cause of Ahab's vengeance.

And, of course, as you read and write, you reread and rewrite, as did John in making more complete sense of the essays of Ralph Waldo Emerson:

> In rereading "Self Reliance" I'm getting a much clearer
> view of what Emerson is trying to say. I'm going to use
> this entry to try and break down his thought (and mine)
> so I can organize a bit. First, and most obvious, is the
> line "imitation is suicide." The second time I read this
> I saw much more relation to "The Divinity School Ad-
> dress." . . .

John uses his journal here to think about one Emerson essay in comparison to another, which helps him find themes and larger patterns. He knows from experience that questions about larger patterns are most likely to show up on essay examinations. By doing exploratory writing like this, he also has a head start on any more formal paper he might be required to write.

□

Answering

Sometimes your journal is a good place to try answering questions, those you pose yourself and those posed by your teacher. In the following entry

Robin, a freshman, writes in response to a first-day question: "How do you learn?"

> I learn through reading which gives me a general de-
> scription of a subject and gives me the tools to begin
> discussing that subject. Once I have a basic idea I
> learn best by watching . . . and talking about the sub-
> ject with another person. I learn and remember best
> through exciting experiences such as my trip to
> Jamaica. . . .

Later in this same journal, Robin writes her way to an answer about whether or not the world of Edgar Allan Poe was a *real* world:

> Haven't we all at one time or another experienced a nag-
> ging conscience from guilt or shame ("Black Cat")? And
> isn't the external appearance of someone or something
> often a reflection of the inner person's feeling or at-
> titudes ("House of Usher")? So, even though these hor-
> ror stories were gruesome and sometimes difficult to
> comprehend, I think Poe in his own way was trying to tell
> us something about his feelings and something about the
> real world.

Robin's *answer* comes from relating her experience of reading Poe to some-thing (she doesn't tell what, nor need she) that she has experienced in the past. By connecting *through writing* Poe's fiction to her own reality, she increases both her understanding and her chances of remembering later what she has read. And by inserting the parenthetical notes, she reminds herself (and shows me) what she was thinking about—a useful reference to have a few weeks from now, when the specific idea that prompted this entry has faded.

□

Asking

Throughout the course of our normal day, we run a lot of questions and problems through our head, most having to do with things that bother us personally, some having to do with what we are studying. Keeping a journal provides a place to collect these questions (both personal and academic), to articulate them precisely, and with luck, to lead answers. Recording such questions provides you with a focus for your reading and something to talk with teacher or classmates about. In the following exam-ple, Marcia generates questions from her reading of *Walden:*

> I was rather confused at the beginning of this chapter.
> What is the deal with the conversation between the Her-
> mit and Thoreau?
>
> What really caught my attention was the specific de-
> scription of the fight between the black and the red
> ants. In this chapter is Thoreau trying to put his
> friends (wild animals) on the same line as those people
> in the village?

Marcia uses her journal to wonder about what she reads. The more she does this, the better will be her chances of asking for clarification in class or, better still, of writing her way to her own answers. In journals, it's a good idea to write "I'm confused" when you are—and to take guesses at resolving that confusion. I often suggest that my poetry students use their journals to write about the lines in the poem they *least* understand—which, of course, usually leads to some kind of understanding.

At other times the journal will serve as a place to think through questions posed by your teacher before you need to make a public statement. In the following example, I asked another one of those first-day general questions to find out how my students would define "the humanities"; here is how Jennifer started her journal entry:

> A definition of the Humanities? Kind of a tough ques-
> tion. I really didn't have any idea before class dis-
> cussion today. A dictionary definition probably
> wouldn't help either. They never do. So I guess by
> remembering what was said I'll have to think of some-
> thing myself. . . .

Notice that this journal writer uses her natural voice, almost like her speaking voice. We think best in comfortable language, so I'm pleased that Jennifer will give the thinking all her attention and let the language take care of itself.

□

Seeing

Writing about what you see helps you see it better. This is true of a scientist in a chemistry laboratory, a biologist out in the field, or a literary scholar examining texts line by line. Writing the observation (1) focuses it, (2) makes the sighting more precise, and (3) actually pushes the visual toward the conceptual.

In the following entry, Richard responds to my question about the nature of the detail on the first page of the Edgar Allan Poe story "The Fall of the House of Usher":

> The mood of the entire first paragraph is such that we feel the impending doom of this guy's situation. Even in the first sentences he seems to be buried, in a sense, in his own living tomb—dark, dreary, soundless, the clouds hanging over him "oppressively." His first glance at the house of Usher leaves such a sense of horror, with its bleak walls and eye-like windows. . . . What stood out to me most though was his personification of the house. . . . Roderick Usher pretty much mirrors the house, and all those descriptive words about the house hold true for Roderick as well.

By writing out both paraphrases and direct quotations of what he found on the page, Richard "sees" that page better. Even if he never rereads this entry, writing it out has increased his chances of understanding and remembering that Poe passage for a long time to come. A good exercise? Write all you can in your journal about what you find on the first page of a novel, story, or essay. It's a good way to train yourself to read closely.

□

Connecting and Extending

One of the best things you can do with journal writing is look for connections to other ideas, themes, and authors studied in the same course. In the following example, David reacts—tongue slightly in cheek—to a specific line in Walt Whitman's "Song of Myself" by comparing him thematically to Emerson, whom we had studied some weeks before:

> Now here's a good one: "Divine am I inside and out, and I make holy whatever I touch. . . ." How about a footnote there? Haven't I heard that "we are all divine" spiel somewhere before?! Hey, Walt, didn't I see you at last month's Harvard Divinity School graduation when Emerson gave that wild speech? This guy moves himself right in with the transcendentalists.

The connection here is a good one, of course, since Whitman was in fact heavily indebted to Emerson for his central ideas—including the divinity of humankind.

Another kind of connection occurs when you use your literature journal to comment on your other classes. Sometimes you will see parallels between the history, philosophy, religion, and literature of a period, such as those which existed in Concord, Massachusetts, in the 1840s and 1850s.

At other times the connections will be less central, but the act of regular writing will help you see them. In the following entry, Sam reflects on his learning in a business class before going on to write about Benjamin Franklin:

> I can't believe how time consuming my BSAD 60 (account-
> ing) class is. The teacher knows his stuff but he goes
> way too fast. It reminds me of what we talked about in
> class yesterday. It's hard to learn if you have to write
> and think at the same time. Back to Ben. . . .

You don't keep a literature journal for purposes of writing like this, but sometimes a quick reflection clears your mind and lets you concentrate better on the business at hand—in this case, paying attention to Ben Franklin.

□

Rethinking

Journals can help you see and re-see your own ideas, and in the process help you to modify and extend them in new and different directions. Look at Bobby's entry as she tries to make sense out of Emily Dickinson's poem "I Heard a Fly Buzz When I Died":

> Boy . . . I was on the wrong track with Emily Dickinson
> completely!! Completely!! I was—I felt rushed and sum-
> marized her—how ridiculous. I didn't even read this
> poem on page 111. . . . It helps so much to try to take a
> poem literally—first. I was jumping to profound con-
> clusions.
>
> OK. So in this poem nothing happens. Nothing happens in
> the sense that she doesn't get at enlightenment as ex-
> pected. You know she is rather anxious for this expecta-
> tion but fails at following it through. I cannot believe
> how much there is in this little poem. She ends her poem
> pessimistically, yet . . . she begins it optimistically
> because of her anxiety to reach her enlightenment—her
> death.

Sometimes the act of writing an observation in your journal causes you to rethink on the spot. You read your own words and see them from a distance not possible when they float loosely in your head, and sometimes you simply take them back, muttering "That's not what I meant at all." For example, Trey wrote the following as he analyzed a short story by Edgar Allan Poe:

```
The first thing that struck me about "The Black Cat" was
Poe's opening paragraph. Poe has this quirk about tell-
ing us that what he is about to say is so horrible that
it's extremely hard to believe. Well, I think it's un-
necessary because in the first place it didn't really
happen. So we're going to believe just the same with or
without the opening paragraph.

Wait a minute, I don't know what I just wrote. I think
that paragraph does a lot, it explains the narrator's
feelings now so when we go back in time we understand the
narrator more. ANYWAY, in the story Poe did some amazing
things. . . .
```

Both Bobby and Trey were prolific writers; each of their journals approached two hundred pages. By making the writing part of their daily routine, they increased the chances of both catching and generating insights about whatever they chose as topics.

□

Conversations

If you are asked to keep a journal by a teacher, chances are she or he will look at it occasionally to see your concerns, and whether or not the class is making sense to you. You can use the journal as well to initiate a dialogue between you and your instructor about things that do concern you but that you haven't time to talk about in person. Here is a snatch of conversation that occurred between Missy and me in an advanced writing class:

MISSY: Look, I want to learn to write well. I want to squeeze as much learning out of this class as possible. Because it means something to me and I care a lot about it. I'm not motivated—at least not like this—by a grade. O.K.? Is the air clear? I want to learn as much of this stuff as I can and semesters are short! So I write hard and I think hard about it a lot . . ., and need the same degree of feedback.

TOBY: Fair enough. You write seriously in here and I'll write seriously back. I agree with you. Too much so-called dialogue between teacher and student is perfunctory or required or something other than real talk shared between people thinking and learning together. Thanks for the candid note!

Sometimes students give me suggestions in their journals, often about the way I'm handling some assigned reading. In Bill's American literature journal, I found this entry:

> Before starting to write on *Moby Dick*, I would like to
> make a special request . . . that you maybe give a second
> thought to assigning a 500 page book like *Moby Dick* in
> the last few weeks of classes.

Bill actually expressed this sentiment aloud in class, and as a class, we talked it through. In truth, next time I assigned *Moby Dick* I *did* think twice about assigning it late in the term and moved it up a week in the schedule. Of course, journals are not letters; they are written primarily to oneself. But in the somewhat artificial learning environment called school, they may accomplish some of the expressive communication between teacher and student usually reserved for the more formal medium of letters or the more informal one of talk.

□

What Journals Look Like

Here are a few suggestions for keeping a journal. Keep in mind that a journal is, fundamentally, a collection of thoughts captured at different moments in time. Remember too that a teacher who requires a journal may want it to be done in a particular way. If not, here are some suggestions that work well:

1. Buy a small looseleaf notebook and divide it into several sections. Use one section to collect your reading notes; use another to write whatever else you are thinking about the course, reactions to class discussion and the like; use yet another section for personal ideas, reflections, and feelings that have nothing to do with the course. If you like, make up other sections for things like scrapbook clippings, profound observations about other classes, and any other categories of ideas you want to keep track of or wrestle with. I like the partitions in my journal because they help me organize my thoughts and my life; yet I know others insist on keeping all the entries together, the unifying principle being simply the chronology of the dates.

2. Write often, regularly, and at length. I write as frequently as I can in my journal, sometimes in the morning with a cup of coffee, sometimes before I go to bed. I intend to write every day, but often that doesn't work out: sometimes I skip a day; other days I write twice. I have learned that the habit of regular writing increases my chances of finding and developing ideas, but it's a haphazard process. Sometimes I think I have a lot to say and nothing much comes out; sometimes I start to write strictly from habit and surprise myself with good ideas. Authors like Ernest Hemingway disciplined themselves to write daily, regardless of inspiration, for essentially the same reason: the discipline will make it more likely that if something is there, you'll find it. I give myself a full

new page for each entry, if only to suggest that I have lots of space with which to play.

3. Write in your most natural voice. The journal is the place where a writer can relax and concentrate on *what* she or he is writing about rather than *how.* There's a good reason for this: the degree to which we worry about matters of form, grammar, mechanics, or style is the degree to which we are distracted from the naked thought before us. Worry about clean, nice-looking, organized language in other places; in the journal, stick with what matters most to you as a thinker and writer.

4. Write double entries. A wonderful idea described by Ann Berthoff in *Forming, Thinking, Writing* (Hayden, 1978) is the double-entry notebook. It works like this: write only on the right-hand pages of your journal; keep the left page blank. Periodically—once or twice a week—return to your earlier entries and comment on them, expanding, modifying, arguing as the purpose suits you. In other words, on left-hand pages adjacent to right-hand entries, write about your former writing and develop a dialogue with your past self. It's amazing to see how ideas change even within the span of a week, if we make writing a regular habit.

5. Index your journal. A former teacher, Dixie Goswami, taught me this trick. At the end of the semester, put in page numbers, titles for each entry, a contents, and write an introduction. This will make your journal a nice-looking, organized document to share with a professor—if he or she wants to see it—but the real purpose is once again for yourself. The act of reviewing and organizing the journal takes you once again through nineteenth-century American or seventeenth-century British authors, now from more distance. Rereading and re-seeing your journal in this fashion is quite simply one of the best synthesizing activities I know of to prepare well for both final examination and further literary study.

One final note: Journal writing is essentially whatever you make it. Of all the modes of writing described in this book, this one gives you the greatest freedom to make it what you want. If you are studying literature, you will probably write a lot about your reading; if you are studying composition or creative writing, what you write about will be virtually unlimited. In any case, the journal is your territory—explore it, map its boundaries, and cultivate it well.

CHAPTER 2

Responding to
Fiction

Arthur W. Biddle
and Allen Shepherd

□

Once upon a time . . .

We all love stories. A tale told around a fire at the mouth of a cave
captivated the human spirit at the very beginnings of language. People are
no different today. Each year thousands of stories are produced for film,
stage, and television. Millions of parents all over the globe still enchant
their children with "Once upon a time" tales.

If stories are so basic to human nature, why do we have to study them?
And just what do we mean when we say we "study" a story?

We study or analyze any work of literature to understand it better—
what it says and how it says it. To discover how the piece is put together
and to grasp the relationship of the parts to the whole. To see the work
in contexts of history, gender, culture. To understand why the story affects
readers as it does. And in a very real way, to participate in the creative
process of making a piece of fiction. The active reader often has a conversation with a text and, through that text, with the author. The reader asks

27

questions of the text and then looks for the answers the text may give. For example, how will the heroine escape from captivity? What does the author mean by "goodness"? What is the effect of telling this story in the present tense? Through this sort of conversation, the reader in fact helps to create the text.

Before we turn to the nature of fiction, we need to consider for a moment the first of a number of terms commonly used in talking about the genre. The term is *persona*, which means literally a mask like those actors wore in ancient Greece. In literary study, *persona* refers to a second or invented self created by an author and through whom the story or poem is presented. In this chapter, two authors—colleagues and friends of many years—have invented a persona to talk about fiction. That persona is the "I" you will see and hear from in the pages that follow.

□

The Nature of Fiction

Fiction today is surely the most natural, familiar, and accessible of literary forms. Like other art forms, it is also ultimately mysterious, but from the "once upon a time" of childhood, we do *know* about fiction and almost instinctively understand what makes a good story. My own children had very distinct preferences and strong biases in bedtime reading. I could not substitute The Cat in the Hat, which they did not like at all, for Where the Wild Things Are, a perennial favorite. I occasionally tried freelancing and soon learned about desirable characters, acceptable plots, and feasible kinds of conflict. From our preschool years, we are familiar with many aspects of fiction.

Given greater experience and sophistication, our tastes change. We appreciate more of the art of fiction and, more prosaically, we are prepared to investigate just how a piece of fiction—whether short story or novella or novel—actually works. We know well enough the rewards of reading fiction, that it enlarges our knowledge, our experience, our understanding, and our range of feeling. The ideal reader, by Henry James's definition, is the one on whom nothing is lost. That kind of perfection is a tall order indeed; I myself aspire to be attentive, intelligent, and responsible, but of course I don't always succeed.

In order to examine how fiction works, we ought to have a demonstration story. Barry Hannah begins a story I like, "Love Too Long," with these lines:

My head's burning off and I got a heart about to bust out of my ribs. All I can do is move from chair to chair with my cigarette. I wear shades. I can't read a magazine. Some days I take my binoculars and look out in the air. They laid me off. I can't find work. My wife's got a job and she takes flying lessons. When she comes over the house in her airplane, I'm afraid she'll screw up and crash. (9)

By the end of the first paragraph, Hannah has got the reader wondering who this man is and just what's wrong. Clearly the man is desperate, going to pieces, and somehow his wife is involved. She has a job and he hasn't. She's taking flying lessons and he's stuck in the house. From the last sentence, we may wonder whether he is afraid *of* her or afraid *for* her. Probably both. In any event, Hannah has set the hook in the reader—we've got to read on and find out.

What leads most readers to want to read on are *characters* and *plot*. We become interested in characters, the people in fiction, particularly when they are introduced as vividly as in Hannah's story, and we want to know what is going to happen, the significant order of what happens being the plot. In one paragraph, of course, plot doesn't develop very significantly, but already there is enough evidence to distinguish between *story* and plot. Story is simply what happens. Plot is likely to involve causation—why things happen as they do. Thus it seems from the first paragraph that the narrator's desperation is in part attributable to his wife, to her employment and her zooming around overhead. He is also developing, it would appear, a heightened sense of his own insignificance. "I got to be a man," he says shortly (9).

□

Character

Traditionally, character has been regarded as the most important component of fiction. How does a writer go about developing a character in fiction? What we first respond to in Hannah's story is the character's *speech*—the words themselves, the rhythm of the sentences, the state of mind they reveal. The *language* is vivid, colloquial, exclamatory. The *rhythms* are broken, staccato. The disjointed sentences seem to burst forth. We can't presume too much at the outset, but our man's mental state is both complex and recognizable. He is hurt and confused and angry and self-condemnatory. Speech, then, set down as either monologue or dialogue, is a principal means of characterization. We do want to know what people sound like.

Physical description is another effective means of character development. Explicit self-description would probably be awkward to incorporate into a monologue such as "Love Too Long." We do, however, get a few evocative visual details. We see our unhappy husband wearing sunglasses (in the house), probably to hide behind; and smoking a cigarette or, I imagine, a succession of them; perched anxiously on one chair, and then moving to another; with the binoculars perhaps hanging on a strap around his neck; and with unread magazines forming a base for the surrounding clutter.

Given these descriptive details, I am reminded of nothing so much as the last survivor in a fortified post anticipating yet another, this time irresistible, assault. Later in the story Hannah writes a scene of confrontation between our narrator and a (of course) superior antagonist. Hannah writes: "He [the antagonist] was a huge person, looked something like a statue of some notable gentleman in ancient history. I couldn't do anything to bring him down. He took all my blows without batting an eye" (15). Here by inference we see the narrator—his self-image. Again he is looking up, without the protective distancing effect of binoculars or even sunglasses this time, and the enemy is overwhelming, invulnerable, and dismissive. Our narrator, inferentially self-described, is small, unimpressive, and ineffectual.

We have also encountered in this single paragraph two other techniques of characterization: portrayal through *action* and through *gesture.* We have seen that the narrator cannot be still, cannot rest, cannot stop thinking; that he is driven, obsessed. His looking up into the sky with his binoculars is a *gesture* which suggests that the answers—peace, ease, happiness—reside with his wife, who may appear at any moment. All along, of course, we have been privy to his thoughts and feelings. That is, we have come to know his world from the inside.

For the sake of clarity and coherence, I have pursued a single, consistent interpretation of character in Hannah's story. This is not meant to imply that there is just one right way and a whole variety of wrong ways. But I have tried to do what critics usually undertake—to make a persuasive case for my reading of the story, without asserting that it is final or definitive.

□

Plot

Good writers don't need plots that are dramatic or violent or even entertaining to gain and hold our interest. Events at a quiet family party will do perfectly well, and did for James Joyce in his story "Clay." Joyce's story, the account of an elderly spinster's visit to a family for whom she'd once worked, impresses some readers as a rather stale slice of life, in which the innocuous word "nice" dominates, and whose action barely skirts the inconsequential. Other readers discover in "Clay" a succession of carefully understated scenes that poignantly portray the barrenness, lovelessness, disorder, and loss which Joyce represents as the essence of his protagonist's experience. The plot leads to no significant changes in the lives of any of the characters; indeed, Joyce's principal point is that they are all trapped. Maria, the protagonist, is not a very perceptive woman, and thus the epiphany, or flash of intuitive understanding, is reserved for another character, who now sees her painful plight differently. He does not, however, recognize that his own situation is scarcely preferable.

Seldom is plot the most significant component of a story. However, the art of storytelling involves the creation of an entire world, and significant events, dramatic or not, are evidence of a world in motion. Events may cause people to change, and most fiction is dynamic, is about change.

What makes a plot move, what glues the events together, is a kind of tension called *conflict*. Sometimes this struggle of opposing forces is resolved, providing a certain satisfaction for the reader. The tension induced by the conflict is eased and some sort of balance and order restored. The point at which one opposing force overcomes the other and the conflict is resolved is the *climax*. Not uncommonly, however, fiction is open-ended, without definitive resolution. The narrator of "Love Too Long" never does achieve dependable understanding, let alone a happy ending. "I'm going to die from love" are his last words, as Hannah completes the circle (15).

One of the opposing forces involved in conflict is likely to be the central character. The other force, or forces, which may be essentially external or essentially internal, include (1) another character or group of characters, (2) the forces of nature or the power of the universe, (3) society or culture, and (4) an aspect of the character's own personality or value system. Given that Hannah's narrator seems somewhat paranoid, we may conclude that his own personality is a significant source of conflict; certainly other characters stand in his way, literally or metaphorically, and his joblessness may reflect social adversity. We may even detect Nature's opposition when the narrator tells us that he is light and nimble and good at elevated construction work, "but the sun always made me sick up there . . ." (10).

□

Point of View

One of the crucial decisions a writer makes is which *point of view* to use in telling a story. You may have been taught that there are only two options: "first person" and "third person". First person features an "I" who is a character in the story he or she tells. Remember how Hannah's story begins—"My head's burning off and I got a heart about to bust out of my ribs"? For reasons we'll explain shortly, we prefer the term *character narrator*, rather than first person narrator, to describe this method of narration.

Critics commonly believe that the use of the character narrator creates a sense of immediacy or authenticity, of a story being conveyed directly. The character narrator may see and know only what is humanly possible. Such a narrator, that is, cannot read other characters' minds or know what is happening a mile away. He or she may speculate endlessly, as Hannah's

31

protagonist does, but cannot be sure of anything and may be deceived. For the writer and for the reader as well, this mode of narration has the advantage of consistent focus, keyed to a single individual's experience. Hannah's use of the character point of view enables us in some measure to share our narrator's perspective, to wonder with him, to endure his distress.

But how does a writer influence the ways we respond to or judge such a narrator? In "Love Too Long," for example, does Hannah make us think the narrator really knows what he's talking about, that he is a man whose experience and intelligence and perceptiveness we can depend on? The answer seems to be yes, with some qualifications: Although there are a good many things the narrator does not fully understand, he *knows* that he does not understand.

Character narrators lacking that self-knowledge may be unreliable witnesses to their own lives. Such an unreliable narrator may be blinded by the limitations of personality or by youth and innocence. One such naive narrator is Huckleberry Finn. Huck greatly admires some poetry that Mark Twain clearly thinks is terrible. The poet, Huck tells us, kept a scrapbook and "used to paste obituaries and accidents and cases of patient suffering in it . . . and write poetry after them out of her own head. It was very good poetry." After quoting an awful poem, Huck says of the poet, Emmeline Grangerford, "She didn't ever have to stop to think," which pretty well nails down the point (87). In employing an unreliable narrator, the writer is really communicating with us over the narrator's head, using a variety of irony. That is, we and the author know and understand things that this character narrator does not. We know, for instance, that writing of any quality requires a lot of thinking.

Instead of using a character narrator, a writer may decide to employ the *omniscient* (or third person) point of view. In eighteenth- and nine-teenth-century novels a common technique is total omniscience, in which the story is told as if it were seen through the eyes of God. The totally omniscient narrator, if so inclined, may know and tell all. For instance, this is how Arnold Bennett's *The Old Wives' Tale* begins:

> Those two girls, Constance and Sophia Baines, paid no heed to the mani-fold interest of their situation, of which, indeed, they had never been conscious. They were, for example, established almost precisely on the fifty-third parallel of latitude.(3)

Here is a narrator who knows with remarkable exactness both where on the map the girls live and what it is they have never known about their own situation. That is to say, the narrator knows what's inside and what's outside, what exists and what doesn't.

This sort of omniscient narrator will on occasion even address the reader, as in this passage from *The American:* "The gentleman in whom we are interested understood no French, but I have said he was intelligent, and here is a good chance to prove it." (5) Henry James's omniscient narrator uses the first person "I," but, unlike Hannah's "I," is not a character in the story. Instead, he or she appears to be the author's representative or persona. It is because the effects of these "I" narrators are so different that we prefer to drop the terms "first person" and "third person" in favor of the more precise *character narrator* and *omniscient narrator*.

In much modern fiction, the narrator's omniscience is consciously limited. Henry James, for instance, often uses a narrator who is not a character, but then restricts that narrator's presentation to what is perceived by just one of the characters. Many writers have adopted this mode of limited omniscience. Look at how William Faulkner begins his short story "Barn Burning":

> The store in which the Justice of the Peace's Court was sitting smelled of cheese. The boy, crouched on his nail keg at the back of the crowded room, knew he smelled cheese, and more; from where he sat he could see the ranked shelves close-packed with the solid, squat, dynamic shapes of tin cans. . . . (3)

Notice that Faulkner focuses on what the boy smells, where he sits, what he can see. Critics today favor the term *focalization* to describe this use of a character's perspective. The writer may maintain the perspective of a single character throughout a work or may shift focalization from one character to another.

Suppose a writer were to rewrite a story and change the point of view. What would happen? If Hannah's story were recast in the limited omniscient point of view, it would be very different. Why? Because that point of view usually conveys authority, coherence, and comprehension, none of which is apparent in the narrator. Why an author chooses a given point of view is a question well worth asking about a work, for as Henry James noted, point of view is that technical aspect which leads the reader most directly into the central interpretive problems posed by a piece of fiction. For example, pondering point of view in fiction may lead to our determining whose story it is, which character's experience is central. And this in turn helps us decide what the story is about.

□

Theme

What ultimately a story means or is about we may call its *thematic concerns*. How do we go about formulating the thematic concerns of a piece of fiction? What do we look for? Themes in fiction are usually expressed through character, action, and image. Ask yourself what has happened to the principal character or characters. Have they made discoveries? What kinds of changes do you see in their circumstances? Important actions are not necessarily physical or dramatic. Some fiction is more cerebral, and the principal action is intellectual or emotional. Consider what kinds of images predominate in the story—images being the sensory content of the work, whatever appeals to the senses.

Let's try to apply these ideas to a formulation of the thematic concerns of "Love Too Long," to use the story for illustrative purposes one last time. At the end, the man's situation has not changed appreciably. The last line of the story, "I'm going to die from love," very much resembles the first, "My head's burning off and I got a heart about to bust out of my ribs." He has certainly gone through a lot of marital pain and suffering, much of it comically described, and has in the process achieved a greater measure of self-awareness. But this is not necessarily going to change his life. Some of the story's dominant images include the wife flying overhead, the huge person who looks like a statue, and a rotting croquet ball lost in the grass, one of the narrator's self-images.

As our consideration of this story would suggest, the meanings of good fiction are not reducible to simple, explicit statements, handy moral guides or codified popular wisdom. Serious fiction does not offer instruction in the same sense that an editorial or a sermon or a book review does. From this it does not follow, however, that statements articulating thematic concerns are of necessity vague, general, or abstract.

What in the end may be said of the thematic concerns of "Love Too Long" is that Hannah offers us the anatomy of a man whose life is overtly in crisis, whose response to the way things are appears to be compounded of surprise, outrage, and dismay, but who in fact has at some level anticipated much of what is going on, and more grimly, sees it as both inescapable and deserved. Given that this story and a number of Hannah's other writings dramatize variations on these themes, we may well conclude that in Hannah's eyes, the condition is widespread. Finally, the fact that Hannah manages to preserve our pleasure in the narrator's distress says something about his view of the world, the kinds of questions that engage him as a writer, and his mastery of fictional technique.

□

Setting

To simplify and clarify discussions of fiction—how it gets written as well as how it gets read—we are in the habit of partitioning character from plot and plot from thematic concerns, when, as we well know, everything is going on simultaneously and is related to everything else. So it is with *setting,* usually defined as where the story happens, the background against which the action of a narrative occurs. Fair enough, particularly if we add *atmosphere,* which implies mood or emotional aura. But look at the following paragraph, the first in James Joyce's often anthologized story "Araby," which exemplifies how a writer begins establishing setting and atmosphere, but which also contains significant intimations of character and theme.

> North Richmond Street, being blind [dead-end], was a quiet street except at the hour when the Christian Brothers' School let the boys free. An uninhabited house of two storeys stood at the blind end, detached from its neighbors in a square ground. The other houses of the street, conscious of decent lives within them, gazed at one another with brown imperturbable faces. (33)

Curiously enough, it is only with the first sentence of the next paragraph that we can tell what the point of view is to be—"The former tenant of our house, a priest, had died in the back drawing-room." As "our house" suggests, the speaker is a character narrator—an adult recalling his childhood, we subsequently learn.

What can we say of setting and atmosphere as conveyed in the first paragraph? As Joyce scholars invariably remark, the setting is autobiographically derived, Joyce having lived at 17 North Richmond Street and having attended the Christian Brothers' School. It is then, in all likelihood, an authentic re-creation, although such authenticity is unlikely to affect our pleasure one way or another. The child who is about to appear will play out several scenes of a deeply felt adolescent drama within the round of these imperturbable brown faces, as if to a maddeningly unresponsive audience, the houses personifying the decent, unimaginative, God-fearing dullness of their adult inhabitants.

Setting continues to be one of the most significant components of the story. Because "Araby" recounts the classic adolescent experience of isolation, alienation, and unrequited love, it seems wholly appropriate that the setting is developed from the beginning as if it were a series of staged scenes in which our narrator fruitlessly aspired to play an heroic role. But as he will recall at the end, framed by another drearily antiromantic theatrical set, this time an almost empty exhibition hall: "Gazing up into the darkness I saw myself as a creature driven and derided by vanity; and my eyes burned with anguish and anger" (41).

To get a sense of the role that setting plays in a work of fiction, try removing a story from its setting. What happens to the plot and characters if you take *Oliver Twist* out of Victorian London? If you transport Ernest Hemingway's Macomber out of East Africa? Or if you pluck Huck Finn and Jim off the Mississippi River?

Sometimes adapters do remove a story from its setting, often to make a work contemporary. What would happen if you took Romeo and Juliet out of Renaissance Italy? You might end up with *West Side Story,* set in New

York City in the 1950s. If you know the film, consider what the author had to do to make that transformation work. Another set of changes is made when a text is translated from one genre (in this case, stage play) to another (motion picture).

It was Henry James who pointed out how artificial are the boundaries between the elements of fiction—plot, character, setting. "A novel is a living thing, all one and continuous, like any other organism, and in proportion as it lives will it be found, I think, that in each of its parts there is something of the other parts." (15) Sometimes indeed, as in considering the function of the Mississippi River in *The Adventures of Huckleberry Finn,* it is difficult to know whether to begin with character or plot or setting. The river, all 1100 miles of it, is of course the scene of many significant events, but in addition it is so consistently personified and so extensively described, so variously powerful and so habitually present, that it may well be regarded as a central character. The river serves also, metaphorically speaking, as a cord on which beads are strung—that is, as a unifying element connecting the loosely related elements of an episodic plot.

□

Symbolism

Of all the components of fiction, the one that often seems to produce the greatest interpretive problems is *symbolism.* For openers, we should consider what symbols are, how they are identified, and what significance they have. A *symbol* is a figure of speech that combines a literal, concrete quality with a suggestive, abstract dimension. Thus a flag, the Stars and Stripes, is a concrete object that stands for the United States. Symbols are often said to be of two types—the universal and the particular. An example of the universal symbol is the long journey that suggests the course of human life. A symbol of more limited application is the bull, which may be understood to represent a rising and active stock market.

Flannery O'Connor was once asked at what stage of her writing she "put in the symbols." It is an entertaining notion—O'Connor slipping in a symbol every three or four pages—but of course that's not what happens. Symbols are fundamental and functional; they are organically related to all the other components we have been concerned with. It's also true that much first-rate fiction has no symbolic content at all. To assume then, as some people do, that the symbol is hiding there somewhere and can be hunted down is a serious interpretive misconception.

How do you recognize a symbol? Careful reading and common sense are the most important requirements. Only after you feel you fully understand the literal level of the story's meaning and yet sense a pattern of suggestive details, a dimension beyond the literal, will you wish to explore symbolic interpretation. Sometimes symbolic significance is readily accessible through speech, gesture, and action. In Hawthorne's tale "The Gray Champion," the scene is a public gathering in Boston at which frightened colonists face a show of military force ordered by the arrogant royal governor, who is contemplating further oppression. From out of the crowd appears a venerable man dressed in ancient clothes and possessed of great authority. He reproves the governor, foretells his downfall, and reassures the people. In this heroic champion, Hawthorne symbolizes the spirit of New England's liberty.

Or consider a one-page chapter, "The Pipe," in Melville's *Moby Dick*. Ahab, smoking his pipe, stands alone on deck, reflecting on the requirements and consequences of his single-minded determination to hunt and kill the white whale. He finds that he cannot any longer enjoy his pipe and throws it overboard. What Melville, himself a lifelong pipe smoker, may be suggesting in this symbolic act is that Ahab is casting away his serenity, rejecting creature comforts, even denying a bit of his humanity in his quest to kill the whale.

Symbolism in fiction depends for its effectiveness on the reader's making the right associations, understanding the ways in which symbols may expand and deepen meaning. Symbols make good literary sense only when considered in the overall context provided by a piece of fiction. The original Greek word for symbol *(sumbolon)* denoted half of something broken in two. Symbols do not stand for other things, but are themselves part of a larger whole. As an interpreter of symbols in fiction, then, you are concerned with putting things together, with seeing the story in more than one dimension.

□

Style

An author's style has been described as the sum of all the choices made. For our purposes, we'll limit that to choices of words and sentence patterns. Words, of course, may be big or small, abstract or concrete, harsh or gentle, and more. Sentences may be short or long, simple or complex, direct or circuitous, and more. Let me illustrate with a paragraph written by Ernest Hemingway, a writer noted for his distinctive style:

> The taxi went up the hill, passed the lighted square, then on into the dark, still climbing, then levelled out onto a dark street behind St. Etienne du Mont, went smoothly down the asphalt, passed the trees and the standing bus at the Place de la Contrescarpe, then turned onto the cobbles of the Rue Mouffetard. There were lighted bars and late open shops on each side of the street. We were sitting apart and we jolted close together going down the old street. Brett's hat was off. Her head was back. I saw her face in the lights from the open shops, then it was dark, then I saw her face

clearly as we came out on the Avenue des Gobelins. The street was torn up and men were working on the car-tracks by the light of acetylene flares. Brett's face was white and the long line of her neck showed in the bright light of the flares. The street was dark again and I kissed her. Our lips were tight together and then she turned away and pressed against the corner of the seat, as far away as she could get. Her head was down. (25)

The Sun Also Rises

Readers tend to have Hemingway's style pegged—simple words in short sentences. They seldom go beyond that. But look at what can happen when you do. I asked a class to write about the style of that passage. Here's what one student wrote in her journal:

```
The adjectives Hemingway employs have dark corrosive
overtones (the word dark is repeated 4-5 times). The
sentences which describe Brett are very short and sim-
ple while the sentences which tell the setting are very
long and descriptively full of detail. Lots of the words
have geometrical references (square, long line, car-
tracks, etc.). The entire paragraph is styled to imply
the heavy influence of modern technology and the post
WWI industrial age. The adjectives used to describe
people are mechanistic. Everything is in definite
terms: dark/light, close together/far away as she could
get—no variation and no real sympathy for the charac-
ters or the environment. Use of extremes. In the first
sentence the taxi is the subject and as the sentence pro-
gresses the rhythm is long, up and down, etc., like the
taxi ride itself. However, once the sentences deal with
the interaction of Jake and Brett the sentences become
quick and abrupt as if necessarily so for the action
(Jake's kissing Brett) to occur in the first place. The
paragraph is complete in itself; there is a setting, a
rising, climax, & falling action, etc. The style of
landscape mirrors what is going on in Jake's & Brett's
emotions and relationships. Very visual paragraph.

                                           Melissa Denick
```

In her analysis Melissa comments on stylistic elements such as word choice and variation in sentence length. More important, though, she notices the effects of those choices. In other words, she shows us the power of an author's style to project meaning beyond itself—to illuminate characterization, conflict, theme.

Although this is a perceptive piece of analysis, Melissa would—if she were going to write a formal paper on Hemingway's prose style—want to expand and refine her observations. For instance, she might note that he regularly puts his emphasis on nouns, that his verbs are seldom very energetic, and that his adjectives are not very colorful. If all this is true,

Melissa might ask herself where the indisputable power of Hemingway's style comes from.

□

Indexing a Novel

Where did Melissa get all her good ideas about the Hemingway passage? Very likely they developed from her practice of annotating or indexing a novel as she reads, a practice I follow and encourage my students to try. By *indexing,* I mean putting into writing those observations and insights you have about a novel as you read it. Writing becomes the means of capturing a fact, relating it to other elements, remembering it, and making it accessible. You might say that indexing is just a fancy name for note taking. To some extent, that's true—call it taking notes systematically. The purposes are to sharpen your observations, to aid your memory, and to help you find important passages later on when you need them for class discussion, for review, and for writing papers. Some of the following techniques may already be familiar. Others will be new. Try them and see what works for you.

In-Text Notes.   In-text notes are those you write on the pages of the book you're reading, the simplest form of indexing. Some people refuse to write in their books. They were probably too well trained by librarians and high school teachers not to deface public property. I agree that you shouldn't deface public property, but I assume you own the novel you're reading. Take possession of it—make it yours by writing in it. And don't worry about the resale value of the book. You won't want to sell your novels anyway.

So, write in your books, but *don't* use highlighter pens. They mark too much, discouraging discrimination. They don't permit you to tell why a passage is important. You can't write words with them. Writing about what you read, even marginal notes, helps you to understand the text better.

Do underline with a pencil or a ballpoint pen, but not more than two or three lines. For longer passages, save time with marginal brackets or sidelining. Underlining doesn't help you remember better, but it marks places in the text to return to.

Do tell yourself why a passage is noteworthy. Underlining and brack-eting only signal something important. Write a few words to tell what it is. I commonly mark key scenes and speeches, symbols, characters, narrative point of view.

Do develop a simple system of notation using whatever symbols and abbreviations are most useful to you and most appropriate to the ap-proaches you take to your reading. Some abbreviations I often use (perhaps because of the kinds of novels I read and the way I read them) are "L & D" (light and dark), "†" (Christian symbolism), "I" (irony), "POV" (point of view). You can devise your own list.

Do use that blank half page or so at the end of each chapter to summarize your insights. At the end of the opening chapter, for instance, you might write your reactions to the central characters as introduced or your notions of what the novel will be about. At the end of the first chapter of *The Adventures of Huckleberry Finn,* one student wrote:

> Huck—impressions. Lonely, superstitious, funny (but doesn't know it), good-hearted, uneducated. Doesn't want to be civilized, religious, respectable. Admires Tom Sawyer, respectable robber. Q: who else talks like this? See Twain's note on dialects.

At the end of the first chapter of Fitzgerald's *The Great Gatsby,* another student reflected:

> Nick, Tom, Daisy, Jordan, un-named baby, Tom's woman in New York, Gatsby. What sort Nick? Gatsby? Nick visits old friends he doesn't know, Daisy (2nd cousin) and Tom (known at Yale); well suited to each other. Money. Nick walks into ugly pseudo-domestic environment. Daisy: lively, shallow. Tom: physically powerful, life after 21 (and football) anticlimactic, worries about decline of the (white) West.

Although neither set of notes is definitive, they illustrate the kind of thinking worth pursuing: raising questions to answer later; setting down preliminary guesses and suspicions; noting unclear points; listing characters; predicting the direction of the plot; making tentative evaluations. In other words, these readers are talking to the text and to the author. Use this technique—and this space—to pull together your questions and to consolidate your insights.

Endnotes.   Even if you use all the margins (not much to them these days) and all the half-pages left at chapter ends, you'll probably want to practice another kind of notation, one that allows you to organize your observations on a larger scale according to your needs as a reader of this particular novel. Maybe a list of characters and the page of their first appearance. Or a catalogue of crucial scenes. Or an outline of the novel's structure as it unfolds. Keys to allusions or symbol systems, if they apply. I call these endnotes because that's where I write them—on the inside covers and other blank pages at the ends of the book.

Indexing a story or a novel makes reading a reciprocal act, like the give and take of good conversation. The author speaks to you through the vehicle of the novel. Through your notes, you respond. You become truly the co-creator of the text. What we as interpreters of fiction may reasonably hope is to convey the pleasure and instruction that come from reading fiction, to explain how we came to our conclusions, and so to converse with other readers, who may themselves have something to say to us.

□

Works Cited

Bennett, Arnold. *The Old Wives's Tale.* New York: Modern Library, n.d.

Faulkner, William. "Barn Burning." *Selected Stories of William Faulkner.* New York: Modern Library, 1962.

Hannah, Barry. "Love Too Long." *Airships.* New York: Delta, 1979.

Hemingway, Ernest. *The Sun Also Rises.* New York: Scribner's, 1970.

James, Henry. *The American.* Boston: Riverside—Houghton Mifflin, 1962.

— — —. "The Art of Fiction." *The Future of the Novel.* New York: Vintage—Random House, 1956.

Joyce, James. "Araby." *Dubliners.* New York: Modern Library, n.d.

Twain, Mark. *The Adventures of Huckleberry Finn.* Boston: Riverside—Houghton Mifflin, 1958.

CHAPTER 3

Responding to Poetry

Sidney Poger

□

The word final, superior to all

Walt Whitman

One of my colleagues, the poet David Huddle, has written a poem called "Coda," in which he tells of an incident his parents related to him during their twice-a-month phone calls:

CODA
David Huddle

Sons grown and gone, they adopt a mutt
that comes, stays ten years, and learns their ways.
On slow walks that good dog leads my parents
a hundred yards out of the gravel driveway
until a gunshot rips through one day's silence.
My mother and father break into a trot,
even though they are old now, too old to run like
this to the curve of the road and the sight
of fat old Daisy's neck a bloody spout,

42

one spent shell steps away, smoke still spooling,
the backs of two running boys, the one not
carrying the gun looking back and laughing.
They are not strong enough to lift the weight
of their dog. They turn back to the empty house.

Through the hundreds of miles between my house
and theirs, my daughters, my wife, and I
take turns talking with my parents in our
twice-a-month phone call. In our talk we try
to pretend it won't be long before our
visit next summer. I hardly hear how
their words sound; I've lost them and they've lost me,
this is just habit, blood, and memory.
They pause, then they tell us about Daisy,
how she must have walked right up to those boys
before they shot her down. . . . And yes, I am
seeing just how it was. My mother's voice
breaks. I am with you, I want to tell them,
but I manage to say only that I see.

David says that writing about poetry is, like writing poetry, an act of inquiry: in both processes you ask yourself questions and see what the answers might be. The difference is that when you are reading a poem, you have the answers the poet has found to his own questions. Since he has kindly allowed me to examine the various drafts he preserved while writing his poem, I will try to retrace the process David went through, seeking the questions he might have asked himself to determine how he arrived at the words that make up his poem.

When asking himself how to describe the distance between himself and his aging parents, David's first answer was to measure the time it took to drive there:

DRAFT: It takes sixteen hours to drive from my
              house to theirs.

This is good poetic practice, measuring distance in terms of hours. David then turned to the more usual measurement of distance by miles, probably figuring that the large number of miles would be more impressive as well as emphasizing the separation, not the hours needed to get there:

REWRITE 1:   It's more than eight hundred miles from my house
              to theirs.

Both measurements are played off against the speed with which the telephone covers the distance. Then, for one draft only, David tries a flat statement:

REWRITE 2:   There are hundreds of miles between my house
and theirs.

Finally, he places the measurement, still in hundreds of miles, into an introductory dependent clause that contrasts with the telephone in the main clause:

REWRITE 3:   Through the hundreds of miles between my house
and theirs, my daughters, my wife, and I
take turns talking with my parents in our
twice-a-month phone call.

By answering one question, about how to measure the distance separating him from his parents, David has answered a couple of others: contrast between distance and communication, between parents at one end and himself and wife and children at the other, between my house and theirs.

These revisions are clear and relatively easy to follow. The questions are direct and indicated by the answers. More difficult to trace are the revisions to the last line. David struggled more to find his answers. His problem was how to make these lines sound right, how to make them fit. David wants to tell his parents how he feels about the severe disruption of their lives, but finds it difficult to express his sympathy over the telephone. At first David concludes the poem with how much he could sympathize with his parents' tragedy:

DRAFT 1:   this seeing the one measure of my love.

Then he measures his distance from his parents through his extension or holding back of sympathy:

DRAFT 2:   Always I can choose
just to listen or to try to see it all,
every choice a measure of love.

Then the choice becomes more specific;

REWRITE 1:   Always I have a choice,
accept the blur of facts or imagine it all,
choosing to see a measure of love.

David's next answer is a direct empathy with his mother's distress and then the distancing of the goodbye:

REWRITE 2:   And yes, I am
       seeing everything. My mother's voice
       breaks off. I am with them! I am with them!
       We say goodbye. We say take it easy.

Apparently that conclusion, with its distancing through the easily repeated cliché of farewell, was not the answer. Still, David struggled with his choice, with what he wants to say and what he can say:

REWRITE 3:   My mother's voice
       breaks. *I am with you,* I want to tell them,
       but instead I murmur, *I see, I see.*

David tried one more answer, by interposing the phone between himself and his parents, essentially comforting the phone and not them:

REWRITE 4:   And yes, I am
       seeing just how it was. My mother's voice
       breaks. I am with you, I want to tell them,
       but I tell the thing in my hand that I see.

But this seems to be too much. David is not writing about how the telephone gets in the way, but how time and distance do. And so the telephone disappears, replaced by the strivings of the poet to say both what he feels as well as what he says to express those feelings:

REWRITE 5:   And yes, I am
       seeing just how it was. My mother's voice
       breaks. I am with you, I want to tell them,
       but I manage to say only that I see.

This process of writing poetry resembles what we do when we read poetry. David has asked himself a series of questions that come under the general question, How can I communicate what I feel in words? The answers he finds, provisional and temporary as they may be, help him to ask further questions whose answers clarify even more what he wants to express. Reading the poem helps us to see what answers David found. In asking ourselves what questions these answers were meant to satisfy, we duplicate David's process of writing the poem. When we compare David's answers with those we might have framed, we see how skillfully David has proceeded and we see whether these answers fit in with our experience.

This double process of exploration, of finding our way back through the answers the poet has provided to the questions he set out to answer, as well as to see how the answers fit in with our experience, is how poetry is written and written about. But if all this seems so straightforward, what makes us so nervous when we are asked to consider a poem and write about it?

Poetry can be daunting. We don't read writing like this very often, we don't talk this way, and many students contend that nobody likes poetry anyway. But even those who twitch nervously before reading a poem admit that, since poetry is made up of words, and words communicate something, we should be able to discover how the poem works, write something about the poem, and find out what we think about it.

□

The Nature of Poetry

Poetry insists on the word. With other forms, plot, character, and point of view are primary considerations. In poetry, the word comes first. In other forms we want to know what happens next: Will the king regain his throne? Will the young lovers be united? Will the murderer be discovered? Poetry insists that we read not only to get to the end of the work, but also to enjoy the trip.

But what exactly makes poetry different? Consider the following sentence: "So much depends upon a red wheelbarrow glazed with rainwater beside the white chickens." Now consider it as the poet arranges the words in a pattern on the page:

> so much depends
> upon
>
> a red wheel
> barrow
>
> glazed with rain
> water
>
> beside the white
> chickens. (38–39)

William C. Williams

This new arrangement sets off the words so that each one becomes important, so that we read each word to see how it fits in with the others and what they all mean together. The four stanzas of Williams' poem present three sharply colored details of red, glazed, and white, which fill our mind.

These stanzas literally depend on the first, as they hang below it on the page, but that stanza depends on the details; "so much" is left ambiguous, in contrast to the concrete words of description, so that we can wonder about the difference between the sharply defined bits of the picture and the ambiguous things which depend on it. Rather than reading the sentence to get to the end to see if we understand it, we read the poem to see the tensions and interactions of its parts.

Poetry repeats certain sounds for the fun of it:

> When blood is nipp'd, and ways be foul,
> Then nightly sings the staring owl;
>
> > > Tu-who;
>
> Tu-whit, to-who—a merry note,
> While greasy Joan doth keel the pot. (V ii 924–28)
>
> > > > *William Shakespeare*

Shakespeare's description of winter doesn't portray snowdrifts or skiing by moonlight. It compares the merry song of an owl, singing in the cold night when the circulation of blood is nipped or constricted, with the work of Joan, who has to scrub the pot and gets covered with grease. This picture of domestic practice is in contrast with domestic, familiar Nature. At the same time, the sound of the words is in itself a pleasure.

We should simultaneously consider what is communicated in a poem, as well as how it is communicated. It is the *how* that often makes us nervous. Surely such a small poem as "The Red Wheelbarrow," which takes up only eight lines, cannot have all those things in it which call for a ten-page analytical paper. We feel the author could not have intended us to go over it so carefully, no matter what our instructor says, and even if we could, what we might find out is going to be thin cheese indeed.

How do we deal with those particulars in order to find out not only how the poem works, but how it works in order to develop meaning? In response to this question, Richard, a student in my modern poetry class, wrote the following about Yeats's "The Song of the Happy Shepherd," illustrating Yeats's theme, "Words alone are certain good," through his own attention to words:

Against the backdrop of mortality painted throughout the poem, Yeats uses a statement and its repetition to assert the value and immortality of words. "Words alone are certain good." Even though the glory of "the kings of old time" is now but "idle words," they still exist even though the kings and the world they ruled are gone. This gives us the image of the all-powerful word that stands alone under its self-generating power. Even the "wandering earth," giving us the image of nature as directionless and chaotic, "may be only a sud-

```
den flaming word / In clanging space a moment heard /
Troubling the endless reverie."
```

The image of "the word," according to Richard, seems to amount to a value that the poet associates with the worth of his work. The power of kings and even of the earth itself are mere words. In the confusion of dreams and the search for truth, Yeats seems to say that words, even by themselves, have enormous power. Of course, the repetition of this statement ("Words alone are certain good.") adds to its force and establishes this idea as a main theme.

Good poems are often dense; they contain a great deal of matter to be tasted, chewed, and digested. Poetry often says complex things with a minimum of words because the author pays attention both to the words and to their patterns. The poet relies on both *denotation,* what the word means, and *connotation,* what the word suggests. English is particularly fortunate in having an enormously rich vocabulary, having borrowed words from more sources than any other language. It has a great storehouse of synonyms, words whose connotations suggest wholly different contexts. If someone asked, "Were you in a fight last night?" you might answer: "No, I was in a *fracas.*" Or in an *argument,* or in a *donnybrook.* Each of these positive answers defines more carefully what the speaker wants to convey about what happened.

□

The Techniques of Poetry

A poem is so compressed that, if everything is considered that can be considered, you will never run out of things to write about. In all forms, good literature is not exhausted through any single interpretation. Each time you write, you support your own interpretation and marshal all the evidence you can to support it. Without finding out all you can, you cannot know what is relevant and make the strongest case for your own interpretation.

Rhythm

Among the important devices peculiar to poetry is *rhythm,* the rise and fall of stress. In English words of two or more syllables, stress one of those syllables (*pen* cil, *tel* e phone, re *solve*). Poets often arrange these stresses in patterns of repetition, patterns with Latin names like *anapest* and *dactyl.* Samuel Taylor Coleridge demystifies these terms in his little poem "Metrical Feet: Lessons for a Boy":

Trochee trips from long to short;
From long to long in solemn sort
Slow Spondee stalks; strong foot! yet ill able
Ever to come up with Dactyl's trisyllable,
Iambics march from short to long;
With a leap and a bound the swift Anapests throng. (401)

A *foot* is the basic rhythmic unit, usually consisting of one stressed and one or two unstressed syllables. George Herbert plays with a variety of these traditionally measured lines in the first stanza of his poem "Easter Wings":

> *Lord,* who createdst Man in wealth and store,
>> Though foolishly he lost the same,
>>> Decaying more and more,
>>>> Till he became
>>>>> Most poore.
>>>> With thee
>>> O let me rise,
>> As Larks, harmoniously
> And sing this day thy Victories.
Then shall the fall further the flight in mee (223)

This stanza goes from 5 to 4 to 3 to 2 to 1 foot per line and then back again in lines predominantly set in iambic feet. In this poem, Herbert represents a bird (turn the stanza on its side to see the bird) which settles to earth as it loses faith in God and then takes off again as it regains that faith, a movement represented as well by the shape of the poem.

In the last hundred years rhythm has become less strictly traditional, freer, and thus more difficult to measure. What is most important is the way in which the rhythm is continued or broken or tampered with in order to emphasize certain words and ideas. Even more traditional poets shift rhythm around to emphasize specific words, as John Milton does in his sonnet "On the Late Massacre in Piedmont":

> Avenge, O Lord, thy slaughtered saints, whose bones
>> Lie scattered on the Alpine mountains cold,
>> Ev'n them who kept thy truth so pure of old
>> When all our fathers worshipped stocks and stones,
> Forget not: in thy book record their groans
>> Who were thy sheep, and in their ancient fold
>> Slain by the bloody Piemontese that rolled
>> Mother with Infant down the rocks. Their moans
> The vales redoubled to the hills, and they
>> To Heav'n. (198)

[UNDERLINING INDICATES EMPHASIS.]

49

Through rhythm as well as through repetition of the long *o* sound, Milton emphasizes the idea of revenge, the slaughtering of the innocents, and the admonition "Forget not." Even the moans of the victims are doubled through their echoes from the hills, which are carried to the Lord, who will avenge their deaths. Similarly, Huddle emphasizes the opening words of his poem, "Sons grown and gone," in order to stress the idea of his parents being alone.

Rhyme

Modern poets also use repeated sounds in new as well as in old ways. Most of us recognize rhyme, the words at the end of lines that repeat the last stressed vowel and all following letters *(moon, June, spitoon, honeymoon)*. These are arranged in patterns the listener recognizes and appreciates. A rhyming couplet may call attention to itself in order to emphasize some conclusion, as when Huddle describes how his relationship with his parents has dwindled into habit before its sudden painful revivification:

> I've lost them and they've lost me,
> this is just habit, blood, and memory.

Poets now tend to use, more and more, *slant rhymes,* which may have the same vowel sound and different consonants (*break, stare*), or the same consonant sounds with different vowels (*thing, slang*). Such rhymes call attention to themselves and to their lack of perfect fit. Dean, another student, discovered how different rhymes make different meanings in Yeats's "The Fisherman":

> When [Yeats] mentions the reality of the world he uses
> some rhymes that are not perfect, whereas when he is
> talking about the fisherman his rhymes are better. For
> example when addressing the reality he rhymes "loved"
> and "reproved," and "hate" and "seat." He seems to be
> stating through these imperfect rhymes that reality is
> imperfect, whereas when he talks about the fisherman he
> uses perfect rhymes such as "still," "hill," "goes,"
> "clothes." Despite this the fisherman does not exist.

Dean discovers that the world of imagination is more regular and more perfect than reality itself. If neither the fisherman nor his world survives, the world of imagination still springs from the devices of the poem.

Alliteration

One of the favorite devices of poets in English is the repetition of initial consonant sounds, or alliteration, as in "On the bald street breaks the blank day" from Tennyson's "In Memoriam." Alliteration is English's substitute for the wealth of rhymes in a language such as Italian, most of whose words end in a vowel. It is easy to find a rhyming word in Italian, much more difficult to do so in English, a language considered rhyme-poor. Translators of Dante, for instance, have labored under the difficulty of reproducing Dante's interlocking rhyme scheme from *The Divine Comedy* in English. Readers like to hear these alliterations, which not only give pleasure and aid the memory, but also emphasize key words. Huddle uses alliteration in "Coda" to call attention to the line "one spent shell steps away, smoke still spooling." He repeats the initial *g* of *grown* five times in the first five lines. There is only one other initial *g* in the poem, on the word "gun" in line 12, as if the word "gunshot" marks a major turning point.

I asked my modern poetry students to explain what repeated sounds communicate to them. Tom wrote: "Repeated sounds and/or alliteration can help a poem to roll off the tongue in an expressive, sometimes pleasant way." Michelle added: "[The use of repeated sounds] is an art of playing with sound and word." You might say that, with the limited number of sounds in English, sounds would be repeated anyway, but not with such regularity as when a poet shows off his skill in a line like "the murmuring of innumerable bees" by echoing the sound of the buzzing of the bees on warm summer days. Kristen discussed some of the effects of sound on meaning: "The effect of the sound of the language, the repetition of the consonants 't,' 'b,' and 's' and the smooth liaisons of word endings with word beginnings, is bland and somnolent like the rivers themselves. One gets an image of a full, content belly after a person has eaten a satisfying dinner. A relaxed, nothing-can-go-wrong feeling sets in along with sleepiness, which is exactly what the sound and the sense of the first stanza suggests." Kristen has asked what the poem does, then found the answer in imagery which reveals what the poem does on the level of sound. Gail pointed out one use of rhyme and alliteration to underline Yeats's theme in "An Acre of Grass," that, as one grows older, he or she needs more passion to write poetry. She finds the growing passion of the older man reflected in the growing number of musical devices:

> The rhyme scheme of the poem reflects the growing energy of the poem. The first two stanzas contain only final rhyming couplets, but the last two stanzas each have two sets of rhymes. The rhyme scheme gets more lively as the speaker's "old man's frenzy" grows.

> Another element that reflects the growing energy of the poem is the alliteration—it is used fairly sparingly in the first two stanzas, and more than twice as often in the last two stanzas. The effect of this is to increase the tempo of the poem and imbue it with more energy.

Imagery

The poet also uses imagery, language that appeals directly to one of the five senses. Poets try to make readers see, hear, smell, taste, and feel what they are describing. Keats is a master of imagery as he describes his desire for wine in "Ode to a Nightingale":

> O, for a draught of vintage! that hath been
>   Cool'd a long age in the deep-delved earth,
> Tasting of Flora and the country green,
>   Dance, and Provençal song, and sunburnt mirth!
> O for a beaker full of the warm South,
>   Full of the true, the blushful Hippocrene,
>   With beaded bubbles winking at the brim,
>   And purple-stained mouth. (205)

One can see the "sunburnt mirth" of the peasant and the mouth of the glass stained with wine, hear the Provençal song, smell the mustiness of "deep-delved earth," taste flowers and meadows, and feel the coolness of the wine as well as the warmth of the country in which it was grown.

Comparison

We might also notice that poetry contains frequent comparisons: the poet never seems to say anything straight. This is not done to bedevil the reader and provide subjects for papers, but because we only learn about something unfamiliar by comparing it to something familiar. If you taste venison for the first time and someone asks you what it tastes like, you might answer: like beef, but richer and gamier. Although this description is inadequate (another answer might be, go and try it yourself), it shows how one person communicates with another through comparing the new with the old. These comparisons are called *similes* if they include the words "like" or "as" and *metaphors* if they omit them. If the poet says her boyfriend is like an oak, she does not mean that he is 30 feet tall and drops acorns. By mentioning the oak, she suggests qualities of steadfastness, size, protection, and beauty which are not explicit parts of the comparison, but important in what she wants to convey. Sometimes the poet goes out of his or her way, as Emily Dickinson puts it, to tell the truth but to tell it slant. John Donne compares his recalcitrant heart to a piece of glass worked on by a glassblower:

> Batter my heart, three-person'd God; for, you
> As yet but knocke, breathe, shine, and seeke to mend;
> That I may rise, and stand, o'erthrow me, and bend
> Your force, to breake, blow, burn and make me new. (299)

When Robert Frost compares a woman to "A Silken Tent," he does not mention the woman, except in the opening words: "She is, as in a field, a silken tent." Frost's description of the tent, as standing on its own but gently bound to the earth through ties of love, makes the secondary or metaphoric meaning more important than the literal description of the tent.

□

Responding to Poetry

I asked my students what they look for when they read a poem. Sharon responded: "I look first to see what the meaning is. The first level meaning. If that's too difficult I look also primarily for the beauty of the words—phrases that jump out at you, unusual metaphors or striking images." Teri emphasizes language: "When I read a poem for pleasure I look for *colorful* words and *language, movement*—sometimes a story." Debbie and Melissa agree on looking for "how it makes me feel." "Definitely the first and most important thing . . . is its relevance to myself, life, experiences, etc. . . . If the poet is writing about something I have seen, felt, experienced, hoped to experience, it makes that poem more than just words." Richard also talks about relevance, but in different terms; "I look for a satisfying conclusion—does the poem 'click shut,' that is, is the ending strong enough to have an effect on me?"

These are general expectations, but when you study a poem in order to write a paper, the first question you might ask is: How does this poem work? You can begin to answer that question by considering the devices described here. Another approach is to ask the kinds of questions posed in James Holstun's chapter, "Literary Criticism and Theory." But no matter what question you ask in a paper, part of its answer is another question—how does the poem mean what I think it means? Only as the answers to the second question affect the first should they be brought within the compass of the paper. Every teacher groans inwardly when he or she sees a paper that specifies details without discrimination: "The rhyme scheme is ABAB, there are a great number of words that start with 'g.'" Only if the rhyme or alliteration or rhythm affects the meaning should it be mentioned. Gail uses only what is important when she sums up the process: "I prefer poetry that uses concise, firm, concrete images that swoop down and surprise you into thinking."

Diction

The choice of particular words affects how we understand the poem. A teacher of mine used to quote George Lyman Kittredge to his Shakespeare class on Kent's curse on Oswald in *Lear*: "Gentlemen, it is one thing to call a man a son of a bitch; it is another to call him son and heir to a bitch; and it is another thing entirely to call him son and heir to a mongrel bitch." Since a poem is made up of words each of which must be paid attention to, one must consider the kinds of words selected, or the diction; when David Huddle called the dog his parents adopted "a mutt," he is saying something about their relationship to the dog. Are the words difficult, unusual, or used in an unusual or formal way, as in the beginning of Milton's "Lycidas"?

> Yet once more, O ye laurels, and once more
> Ye myrtles brown, with ivy never sere,
> I come to pluck your berries harsh and crude,
> And with forced fingers rude
> Shatter your leaves before the mellowing year. (142)

Are they short, common, and direct, as in Leigh Hunt's poem "Rondeau"?

> Jenny kissed me when we met,
>   Jumping from the chair she sat in;
> Time, you thief, who love to get
>   Sweets into your list, put that in:
> Say I'm weary, say I'm sad,
>   Say that health and wealth have missed me,
> Say I'm growing old, but add,
>   Jenny kissed me. (763)

Are the words meant to resemble the rhythms of everyday speech, or are they meant to distance us from the everyday? Philip Larkin in "Church-Going" begins with an offhand observation of a church

> some brass and stuff
> Up at the holy end

but ends with a serious observation in dignified language to show human-kind's innate respect for the questions religion raises: "A serious house on serious earth it is." (29)

When Gail was writing about Wallace Stevens' "On the Manner of Addressing Clouds," she made some of her discoveries through an examination of diction:

The language of the poem, as in most of Stevens' work, is opulent. He uses magnificent language to write about language: "sustaining pomps," "exaltation without sound," "music of meet resignation." Such gorgeous language is a way of capturing the reader in a situation and making it seem beyond the bounds of everyday experi-

ence. It is as though Stevens strips away the plain layer
of everyday existence to reveal a sensuous world of
sound and language.

Once you have determined the *diction* or choice of words and *tone of voice* or the speaker's attitude toward self, audience, and subject, you have to decide which words are emphasized. This is done not only through examining rhythm, rhyme, and sound, but also through examining how the unit of thought works. Is the unit of thought in the line, in one of Whitman's lists in "Song of Myself":

The carpenter dresses his plank, the tongue of his foreplane whistles
its wild ascending lisp (41)

Or is it the couplet, as in A. E. Housman's "Terence, This Is Stupid Stuff":

But oh, good Lord, the verse you make,
It gives a chap the belly-ache. (209)

Or is it in the stanza, as when Andrew Marvell starts the first verse of "To His Coy Mistress" with a proposition:

Had we but World enough, and Time,

decides in the second stanza that we haven't

But at my back I alwaies hear
Times winged Chariot hurrying near:

then comes to a conclusion in the third stanza:

Now therefore . . . (1090–91)

Is the thought expressed through direct or indirect comparison (metaphor or simile) or through an implied comparison, as when Ralph Waldo Emerson uses architectural terms in the second stanza of "The Snow Storm":

Come see the north wind's <u>masonry.</u>
Out of an unseen <u>quarry</u> evermore
Furnished with <u>tile,</u> the fierce <u>artificer</u>
Curves his white <u>bastions</u> with projected <u>roof</u>
Round every windward <u>stake,</u> or tree, or <u>door.</u> (42)

[EMPHASIS ADDED.]

Are there forms which control the shape the thought takes, such as the octet and sestet of the Italian sonnet, in which the first eight lines present one thought and the last six present a response, or the three quatrains and a couplet of the English sonnet, which presents three parallel ideas and a summary couplet? All these ways of presentation guide us to an understanding of the poem we could not have realized otherwise.

Point of View

The reader must determine who is speaking in a poem. It is never the poet, but some imaginary person. Even if the poet wants to express some of his or her own values, the speaker is never identical with the writer. We have to ask ourselves: Who is the imaginary speaker? Is he or she well educated? Old or young? Serious or frivolous? Serious or funny? The point of view the poet chooses determines the diction, and the diction reveals the values of the speaker. The poet may urge his dying father to struggle against the onset of death, as Dylan Thomas does: "Do not go gentle into that good night." (128)

The poet may speak almost directly in his or her own voice, as when Milton addresses the reader in order to "justif[y] God's ways to man," which differs from the voice and values of Pope who "vindicates" God's ways. Neither of these voices indicates Milton's position as the great rebel nor Pope's role as a Catholic constrained by a Protestant majority. Huddle may have parents who adopted a dog, whose dog is shot, and may have a wife and two daughters, as I know he does, but the poem does not show his skill at volleyball, his beautiful reading voice, his being as a teacher. The poem shows him only in his role as husband and son, not in all his complex life.

While all forms of literature use dialogue, there are poems that advance like drama through people speaking to each other, changing their minds as they talk out their different views, as Mary and Warren do in Robert Frost's "The Death of the Hired Man." Their two definitions of home, while they both take in the wanderer, do so in very different spirit:

> "Home is the place where, when you have to go there,
> They have to take you in."
> 　　　　　　　　　"I should have called it
> Something you somehow haven't to deserve." (20)

Neither definition is complete without taking the other into consideration, and by the end of the poem Warren has come to adopt Mary's view while she has made room for his. Robert Browning carries off perhaps the more difficult, and more showy, task of suggesting the dramatic action with only one speaker, but one whose speech implies the reaction of that second person, in his dramatic monologues, the most famous of which is "My Last Duchess."

Poets change their voices from poem to poem. T. S. Eliot uses one of several voices in "Ash Wednesday," another in *Four Quartets,* a third, consistent narrative voice or another character in "The Love Song of J. Alfred Prufrock." Eliot warned his reader not to mistake the voice in *The Waste Land* as his own when, in an early version, he titled his poem with a quote from Dickens: "He Do the Police in Different Voices."

Even though poetry may share the descriptive traits of narrative and drama, whose structure is built upon action, poetry has other resources. Poetry probably began as entertainment sung to a lyre, hence the term *lyric.* While the word "lyric" originally described singing, we now apply it generally to those poems, or parts of poems, whose melody impresses us above all else.

Some poems may be built on pure description. In "The Bells," E. A. Poe describes the sounds of various bells and their effects on the reader; there is no story, no narration, no dialogue, no action. The poem proceeds through description, sound, and rhythm. Another poem may deal with some generalized topic, but without applicability to any specific situation, as when Robert Herrick advises young girls to enjoy their beauty while they can in "Gather Ye Rosebuds While Ye May." Of course, you can use songs to persuade to action; after all, Herrick's is one of the most famous seduction poems in the language. But even though you may use this poem as a means to action, its main impulse is to sing something about our condition on earth.

Some call the lyric impulse, the impulse to sing, the purest strain of the poetic, most divorced from the forms of fiction and drama. Admittedly, the lyric voice is difficult to write about since it is allied with song, and music may rise beyond the powers of analysis. But poetry is made up of words, not notes. With a careful examination of what you have read and an understanding of how the poem is put together, you will respond to poetry as it deserves to be responded to: as one of the most polished forms of art.

□

Works Cited

Coleridge, Samuel Taylor. *The Poems of Samuel Taylor Coleridge.* Ernest Hartley Coleridge. Oxford Standard Authors. New York: Oxford UP, 1960.

Donne, John. *The Poems of John Donne.* Ed. Herbert Grierson. New York: Oxford UP, 1951.

Emerson, Ralph Waldo. *The Complete Works of Ralph Waldo Emerson Poems* vol. IX. Ed. E. W. Emerson. Boston: Houghton Mifflin, 1904.

Frost, Robert. *North of Boston.* New York: Holt, 1916.

Herbert, George. "Easter Wings." *Major Poets of the Earlier Seventeenth Century.* Ed. Barbara K. Lewalski et al. New York: Odyssey, 1973.

Hunt, Leigh. "Rondeau." *English Romantic Poetry and Prose.* Ed. Russell Noyes. New York: Oxford UP, 1956.

Housman, A. E. "Terence, This Is Stupid Stuff . . ." *English Poetry in Transition 1880–1920.* Ed. John M. Munro. New York: Pegasus, 1968.

Keats, John. *Selected Poems and Letters.* Ed. Douglas Bush. Boston: Houghton Mifflin, 1959.

Larkin, Philip. *The Less Deceived.* London: Marvell Press, 1973.

Marvell, Andrew. "To His Coy Mistress." *Major Poets of the Earlier Seventeenth Century.* Ed. Barbara K. Lewalski et al. New York: Odyssey, 1973.

Milton, John. *The Complete Poetical Works of John Milton.* Ed. Douglas Bush. Boston: Houghton Mifflin, 1965.

Shakespeare, William. *Love's Labour's Lost.* Ed. Wilbur L. Cross and Tucker Brooke. New Haven: Yale UP, 1954.

Thomas, Dylan. *The Collected Poems of Dylan Thomas.* New York: New Directions, 1953.

Whitman, Walt. *Leaves of Grass.* Ed. Scully Bradley et al. New York: Norton, 1973.

Williams, William Carlos. *Selected Poems.* New York: New Directions, 1963.

CHAPTER 4

Responding to Drama

James Howe

I had to grow into loving theater. I could always absorb poems and stories, so that they became part of me. But plays seemed different—more public somehow, maybe because they're written to be performed. Without stages and actors and actresses, there would be neither play-wrights nor plays. Every printed version of a play is a script waiting to be enacted.

So I had to learn to read them that way—knowing that their final form occurs in the theater, not on the page. And we have to learn to write about them that way too. This chapter will explore what "that way" means for us, first as a theater audience, and then as readers and writers.

□

Drama as Performance

In performance, characters come to life. They occupy physical space, they move, and nearly always they speak. While reading fiction or poetry, we imagine; as an audience for a play, we see and hear.

In some ways, of course, a play is a lot like a novel or short story. Its *action* usually takes narrative form. Its *characters* do things and say things which are consistent with their roles, and these "things" in turn form the *plot,* including the *conflict* (usually between two or more characters, or between two elements within one character). The action of this conflict will intensify to a moment of emotional or intellectual *climax* (or both). At this climax, the two main conflicting elements will confront each other most directly. We will see their nature most clearly, and understand the fictional world most completely.

So in writing about drama, we can usually write about its story. But we must do it differently than we do for other literary forms, and this difference has less to do with its content than with the nature of its presentation.

For example, there is seldom a narrator, even implicitly, to tell the characters' story for them. Therefore, once a performance (or a reading) begins, the *point of view* cannot be changed. We are sitting in the same seat in the same theater during an entire performance of a play, looking always in the same direction at the same stage.

In addition, the plot needs to unfold more quickly than in a novel. The action is often telescoped into extremely concentrated form. In the medieval allegorical play "Everyman," the central character Everyman is confronted by the character Death on the last day of his life. In *Macbeth,* the main character changes from loyal subject to king killer in the very first act; in *Othello,* the hero's rapturous love is transformed by Iago into murderous rage in less than two acts. Indeed, the word "dramatic" is often used in common speech as a synonym for "intense" or "concentrated" effect.

There is a practical reason for this: in the theater, we can only sit so long, and we can only pay attention so long. Unlike the process of reading, which we can do on our favorite couch, picking up our book and putting it down at leisure, in a theater we're stuck for the whole two or three hours in a single seat. We tend to get tired, and our attention starts to drift. So a play has to be forceful and quick-moving, start to finish. It has to have drive.

Another difference between fiction and drama is that dramatic effects are *stage* effects. In novels we are often asked to imagine a particular scene as it might look if it were unfolding in real life. A play, however, is presented on a particular stage. Its visual effects depend on this stage—its size and shape, the nature of the scenery and costuming, even its placement in the theater. For example, in 1600 Shakespeare's stage thrust out into the middle of the audience, and was an open-air platform. No artificial lighting emphasized the separation between actors and audience; an actor literally stood in the middle of his audience. Both were lit in the same way, by daylight. Under such relatively intimate circumstances, the soliloquy—a character speaking his mind directly to the audience—seems more natural than it does in the conventional modern theater, where the stage area is more distinctly set off from the audience area, and where artificial lights emphasize this separation by lighting the players and leaving the audience in darkness.

For the sake of clarity about stage effects, let's take a closer look at Shakespeare's stage. It was essentially a bare stage. The few sets (there was virtually nothing we would call scenery) were symbolic rather than realistic. They represented generic places like a garden, a cave, a mountain, a throne, but not particular places, and they did not have the details usually associated with verisimilitude. Indeed, this stage, like the classical Greek one, was essentially unlocalized; because it didn't represent a particular place, it could be any place, and any time as well.

The effectiveness of our reading of Shakespeare's plays depends on imagining their action on this stage. For example, in Shakespeare's *Henry the Fourth, Part One,* when Falstaff falls in battle "as if he were dead," we must imagine this act from the perspective of the audience at an actual performance. As readers, we know from the stage direction that Falstaff is faking. From the perspective of an audience, though, we don't know about the stage direction; we only know what we see: that Falstaff "falls down as if he were dead." So of course we believe that he is dead. So when Falstaff gets up again a little later, we must imagine the surprise we would certainly experience in the theater. Further, if we see Falstaff as a character who is larger than life, perhaps embodying some basic quality that exceeds our normal human limits (like spontaneity or freedom from conventional codes of conduct), then the surprise may seem almost miraculous. We might even see his return to life as a kind of resurrection, a reaffirmation of the enduring power of a basic life principle.

In addition to the absence of a narrator, the quick development of the plot, and the use of stage effects, a play's presentation differs in one other crucial way from fiction and poetry. The characters have great power simply because they physically act out their own stories. They exist directly before us in our own immediate field of experience. We cannot diminish their presence by arguing, as we can of characters we imagine from reading a novel, that they are not lifelike. In fact, in "reality," when a person is suddenly run over by a truck—or when anything similarly outside our normal range of expectation occurs—we do not have the leisure to pretend that it isn't really happening. Quite to the contrary, we feel pain, we see blood, we hear sirens, and when we try to walk away, we find that our legs don't work. It may be preposterous, but it is also "real." In the same way, we must believe in characters who are palpably before us in the theater.

□

Reading Drama

Of course, in a literature class the script itself is all we have. We must keep in mind that it only seems to be a text, that it is actually a play waiting to be acted. Then we will not look for an authoritative (or even ironic) narrative voice; nor will we evaluate characters and events on the basis of their resemblance to "life." Instead, we will accept what the script gives us and try to imagine it acted on a particular stage. We will read it as if we were directors planning a production. We will read it in the awareness that the play is partly our own creation, that we ourselves mediate between the script and the world (as represented by an audience). At the same time, though, we must imagine it as we would have it played onstage to ourselves as a part of that audience. By giving the script an interpretation and then imagining its effects onstage, we complete it and bring it to life. Indeed, if there is an authoritative point of view, it is ours. As imagined directors, we determine the perspective from which it will be staged.

☐

Writing About Drama

When we write about a play, we present the results of our reading. Therefore, we may write about any of the stage conventions we discussed above and about how a particular play accommodates itself to them. In doing so, we might also have to study how these conventions were used in the past—for example, what kind of stage Shakespeare's theater had—in order to assess how a play's conventions might have worked during its own time.

In literature courses though, most of us will be writing most of the time about those elements of drama which are similar to fiction or poetry. We will be analyzing character, plot, tone (or atmosphere), and language, but always in the awareness that these elements are meant to happen on a stage. And whatever our topic, we will be discussing how it contributes to a final effect, or to an interpretation, of the full play (as we imagine it performed).

Writing About Character

Before our formal writing begins, we must choose a topic. We might decide to analyze the nature of a character (or of the plot or language). So we start collecting information. In a play, most of this information consists of the character's speeches, since there is no narrator to describe either the character or his actions. We study what the character says to figure out what kind of person he is. If, for example, we see that a character never tells a lie, has no sense of humor, never expresses any emotion, and is named Truth, we might think of her as allegorical rather than fully dimensioned and realistic. This is not good or bad; it is simply one dramatic genre rather than another.

A play teaches us how to see it in this way, teaches us what kinds of things to expect. In this example, we might expect a lesson about truth and the way it operates in the world—but we might not expect our strongest emotions to be engaged. Truth is not like us; she does not suffer from pain and confusion and failure, nor feel pride and joy. We do, and we feel most sympathetic to characters who resemble us in these things. Therefore, we might analyze the idea Truth represents, and how clearly and forcefully she enacts that idea, but we probably would not evaluate her on the basis of whether or not she makes us cry. She seems better suited for other effects.

An analysis of the main characters (or of any of the other major elements of a play), then, shows us that play's *conventions*—the kind of effects it seems to pursue. Then at last we can begin to imagine it on a stage.

And when we do imagine it onstage, we see at once how limited characters are. Because there is seldom any clear authorial voice, they can seldom act as their author's mouthpiece. When they step forward to tell us what they think, they speak merely in their own persons; their understanding is limited (as ours is) by temperament and by ability to understand. When Othello asks us to think of him as "one that lov'd not wisely but too well," for example, we must reserve judgment. We know that he's just killed the woman he loves, and then found out that his suspicions about her were wrong. We know that, under the circumstances, he may be slightly unhinged, maybe trying desperately not to lose his noble self-image. Sometimes a character deceives himself; sometimes, though, he may actually be lying. Whatever is happening, we usually have to figure it out for ourselves.

Examples of Character Interpretation

In Shakespeare's *The Taming of the Shrew,* Kate is the shrew: she feels mistreated by her family and by society. She beats up her sister, yells at her father, and breaks a lute over the head of a tutor. Meanwhile Petruchio, who is looking for a wealthy wife, sees that she is not yet spoken for and admires her spirit. Clearly, however, his wooing is going to be a challenge. Kate is extremely suspicious and has no reason to trust her new suitor. So he develops a plan of attack, and it is so successful that many people think he's a bully.

One of my students, Laurie, found this idea interesting, and decided to test it by studying his character. However, she does not take even his most obvious speeches at face value. Rather, she uses them to assess his degree of self-awareness. Petruchio, she writes,

```
. . . proceeds to outline his plan of attack, telling us
he is going to put on an act, put on false appearances, to
tame her:
```

Say that she rail, why then I'll tell her plain
She sings as sweetly as a nightingale. (2.1.170–171)

> He shows us that he is aware [enough] of fronts and plans
> to use one himself.

Laurie looks below the surface of her character's speech. She is interested in Petruchio's plan to deceive Kate, but she is even more interested in how this plan implies that he is self-aware, thus possibly not self-deceiving, possibly even admirable. The rest of her essay tests this hypothesis against Petruchio's acts and other speeches.

Another problem, however, is that our way of seeing a character is probably only one of many plausible ways. This is true again because we must figure everything out for ourselves, and also because every reader "sees" a little differently from every other reader. Thus, while discussing the personality of Kate in the same play, Hilary, another student, makes her awareness of other possibilities very clear. Indeed, this awareness is a challenge, forcing her to sharpen her sensitivity to the character so that she can justify her way of seeing it. In the passage below, Hilary responds differently to Petruchio's apparent bullying when he demands that Kate agree with whatever he says, no matter how wrong:

> Kate's first act of acquiescence, *some might call it
> submission,* comes when she says, "But sun it is not, when
> you say it is not;/ And the moon changes even as your
> mind./ What you will have it nam'd, even that it is,/ And
> so it shall be so for Katherine." (4.5.19-22) Now we see
> that her hesitancy has been replaced by a more mature and
> self-aware assurance. In learning the rules of the game
> from Petruchio, she has become comfortable within the
> boundaries it has created, and she is able to lay down
> her guard and not feel the fool because of it. It is to a
> new level of understanding that Petruchio has led her
> *and not as some might think into a role of submission*
> [italics added].

Rebecca, a third student, exemplifies the cause of this problem, the fact that different readers see differently. She comes to a conclusion very similar to Hilary's, but she gets there from a quite different set of observations:

> Although she [Kate] originally is violent and rude, she
> is also interesting and human. In contrast, at the end of
> the play, she seems artificial and shallow. This dras-
> tic change in behavior leads us to believe that she may
> be pretending.

Therefore,

> . . . she is not tamed; she is taught, taught how to play
> Petruchio's game.

Hilary too interpreted Kate as pretending at the end of the play, but because she seemed truly at "a new level of understanding," not because she seemed "artificial and shallow."

Writing About Language

As we have seen, the language of the characters is all we have to study in a play. However, it can be studied in ways other than in its relation to character. Just as with the characters, however, we must imagine it as it would be in the theater—as we might hear it spoken. We must ask ourselves questions like these: How might this particular character, with this particular temperament, speak this line? How must he or she feel like to say this? And therefore, what might the inflection of this line be? What might the voice sound like here? For example, the fourth act of *The Merchant of Venice* is often thought to be its climax. The vengeful Shylock is tried in a courtroom by the heroine Portia. However, if we remember that a boy actor with a high-pitched voice is playing her role, and that she in turn is disguised as a man, and that she beats Shylock by applying his rules more strictly than he does himself, demanding exactly a pound of flesh, no more, no less, we might see the scene as parody rather than climax. In imagining the effect of language in a play, we must imagine it being spoken.

We might also look for *patterns* of language which run throughout a play. These patterns often reveal larger themes. For example, when my student Rebecca writes about Portia in *The Merchant of Venice,* she focuses on her use of the single word "will" in the first act. Portia "is frustrated because she has no control over who she may marry"; her dead father's will requires her to marry whatever suitor happens to guess the answer to the casket riddle. Rebecca continues:

> She says, "I may neither choose who I would, nor refuse
> who I dislike; so is the will of a living daughter curb'd
> by the will of a dead father" (1.2.23-25). Portia's de-
> sire, her will, is being dominated by the law, a will.
> Shakespeare, by using the word "will" to represent both
> desires and legal documents, reveals that a connection
> exists between these opposing forces. Furthermore, he
> contrasts these forces by associating the word "living"
> with "desires" and the word "dead" with "laws." Already
> we see that desires are more substantial than laws in
> light of the fact that they are alive.

Rebecca's essay goes on to contrast the value of love in the whole play to the value of the letter of the law by which Shylock will try to gain revenge.

Portia's speech shows us where she stands on this issue. The play as a whole teaches us, therefore, how to view Portia.

Interpreting the Conventions of Performance

Sometimes, however, a play behaves unpredictably, in ways quite outside the conventions we have been discussing. And sometimes this violation of convention creates the most powerful effects of all.

Despite the fact that our seats are fixed in a particular place in the theater, and that there is seldom a narrator—or any other kind of superior consciousness—to oversee our reaction to the play, the playwright *can* change our perspective. He can do so by encouraging one set of expectations, then violating them. For example, in *The Merchant of Venice* Shakespeare seems to be writing a conventionally moral play about the values of Christian love and mercy, contrasted with the Jew Shylock's miserliness and desire for revenge. But when the Christians defeat Shylock at the climax of the play, they seem as merciless and vengeful as he. Indeed, the villain seems to become their victim. The expected roles of the conflicting characters are reversed, the expected conventional value system is subverted, and for almost four centuries now the play has remained a puzzle.

Why might a playwright do such a thing?

We have seen how the performance aspect of drama requires complex theatrical conventions. This question about Shakespeare requires us to reconsider the implications of these conventions. When we imagine ourselves in a theater watching a play, we are conscious of imagining ourselves to be in an alien place—a house dedicated to illusion. At the same time, the illusionary characters truly exist; they are physically present before us. We are therefore fully aware of what we do—fully aware that we pretend to believe that an actor really is the character he plays; that a stage with made up scenery really is the place it pretends to be; and that the author's carefully composed language, memorized and spoken by a trained actor, is really the spontaneous, extemporaneous speech of a character.

Having been drawn into the story (having agreed to pretend to believe in it), our emotions are engaged. If we are puzzled by it, we will feel this puzzlement and actively try to resolve it. In essence, by making us think harder, the playwright asks us to see more!

In the case of *The Merchant of Venice,* Shakespeare creates Christian characters with whom we naturally associate ourselves because they seem to represent positive qualities like mercy and love. We cheer for Portia as she defeats the enemy. Then we see that in winning, she and the other Christians show not mercy or love, but delight in vengeance. And we in the audience are forced to question our own virtue—we have caught ourselves cheering the vengeful Christians on! Suddenly the issues of the play become personal. We ourselves are implicated in the hypocrisy of the

Venetians. We must reexamine ourselves in the light of our reaction to the play. In other words, because we are puzzled, we turn inward. As a result, the play strikes us more forcefully—and more meaningfully—than most "conventional" plays.

Similarly, some of the most provocative student essays will address a question like How does this play make me feel? and then analyze the play to answer the follow-up question, How did it get me to feel that way?

In getting us to feel as he or she wants us to, a playwright can undermine our expectations even more completely than we have so far seen. He or she can call into question the most basic conventions of the genre. Luigi Pirandello, for example, creates six characters whose script involves their search for an author and a story so that they can have roles to play. This is important to them because without a role, a character has no identity. In *Six Characters in Search of an Author* there is nothing for us to pretend to believe in. We are therefore forced to see such characters to be pure artifice, lacking even the "reality" of conventional dramatic pretense. As Pirandello's audience, we are compelled to notice this fact because they themselves insist upon it in their speeches. Yet gradually we perceive that in their search for identity onstage, they are not so different from us in our own lives. And when we see this analogy we may ask: Who in fact are *we?* What identity have we that we can count on?

By breaking the expected pattern of drama so that we are forced to disbelieve in it, the playwright makes his or her message about our lives more forceful, not less. The form of drama that functions in this way is called *metadrama* because it is self-referential. It refers to itself as being drama, a thing made by another human being, and therefore a thing which reminds us (unlike more conventional plays) that it is not "real."

Metadrama is powerful because it draws directly on the essential nature of the theater. It refers explicitly to itself as an illusion whose reality is *only* apparent, and insists that its power—the power of theater—is drawn from this fact. Because it is not real, we give it license to portray our frailties more strongly, more appallingly than we would normally allow even our friends to do. And because it is not real, we feel we need not take it too seriously. We need not construct our normal defense mechanisms against it. We need not deny its truth. And so, because it is not real, its power is even greater than most of our encounters with the normal world.

Even when this quality is not written into the script, actors and actresses often emphasize the metadramatic nature of theater. They often find their masks and costumes to be strangely liberating. In their apparent anonymity, behind an assumed role, they can "act out" human impulses and qualities which in normal life must be suppressed, or at least restrained. There is always a tension between the actor's need to hide his "real" identity in order to play a role, and the freedom he feels to express himself through the role. All of us feel jealousy, for example, but few of us would give it the full expression we might sometimes wish. What an opportunity the role of Othello gives us! Metadrama merely makes this theatrical truth explicit.

Perhaps in recognition of this fact of the stage, many playwrights build the tension between acting and being, between the normal limits of acceptable behavior and the gargantuan dimensions of secret desire, into the characters in their scripts. For example, Shakespeare's King Richard III gloats about his ability to fool the other characters. Quite explicitly, he is a character who "acts"—who does onstage in his role what an actor does: he pretends to be different than he is. However, he does so in order to achieve his true desire: to be king. Part of his power is that by acting, he can "stage" the full monstrousness of his desire, and we can marvel at his skill in doing it. Such characters enact the dual quality of our nature too.

One of my students was interested in discovering why, although Richard is a villain, we like him in the early parts of the play. In trying to figure this out, Tammy becomes conscious of Richard as a character who acts, and how this influences her feelings:

> When Shakespeare attaches us to a devious character he
> enables us to take a journey to the darker side of na-
> ture. While doing this, he also sees how far he can push
> our sense of morality. His method of doing so is to
> worsen the character's behavior by degrees until fi-
> nally we can like him no more.

Tammy then focuses on a particular event from early in the play by way of example:

> The scene I'm referring to is usually called "the seduc-
> tion of Anne," but I think it would be safe to call it the
> "seduction of the audience" as well. What's so incred-
> ible about this scene is that the audience doesn't re-
> ally expect him [Richard] to succeed, but he does. He is an
> even better con-artist than we had thought he'd be. . . .
> We can't help but admire the wordplay and manipulation
> on Richard's part, . . .

Later in the play, as Richard's villainy gets worse and worse, Tammy doesn't justify her turning against him from the moral point of view, which would run the risk of imposing her own standards of morality on Shakespeare. Instead, she justifies *her* change by noticing a change in *him:*

> At this point there's no hope for liking Richard. If *he*
> can't live with his conscience, how can *we?* [italics
> added]

Then Tammy moves toward her conclusion, continuing to draw on her self-consciousness about being part of an audience. By the final act,

> Without the shows to suspend our moral judgment we can no
> longer like him, and therefore we have no hero to like in
> this play. We also feel guilty for ever having liked him,
> and even worse, being his accomplice by liking his
> tricks well enough to enjoy his successes.

This consideration of audience response, then, allows Tammy to show *how it feels in the audience* to watch a play that, from an intellectual point of view, teaches a very simple lesson about conventional morality. This approach also allows her to identify the source of the play's power, then analyze the way it realizes that power—the way it draws us in and then forces us to second-guess ourselves.

Even when a play is being enacted as a pretense of "reality," then, its greatest source of power may come from our consciousness that it is meant to be performed. And in imagining its performance, we readers complete the script; we give it a self-consistent interpretation that includes its enactment.

□

Television and Film

Besides drama, there are two other visual media we might also study in a course in literature: television and film. However, because we experience them differently than we do drama, the problem of writing about them is not the same.

The most obvious difference is that although we typically read plays in a literature class, we typically watch television and films. In addition, however, these media are unlike drama because they are not live performances, but are interpreted for us by the camera—an intermediary eye that oversees and, to some extent, interprets what we see. The camera can zoom into a close-up—of a facial expression, a bleeding wound—and can also distance itself to give a panorama: a whole field of battle, a cast of thousands, "real" clouds rolling in from the horizon. The intermediary camera, that is, provides an analogue to the narrative voice in fiction: it can underline a particular perspective or emphasis by the angle of shooting. However, it might be said that the camera's perspective is more dictatorial than the authorial voice of fiction or the director's perspective in the theater. While reading, we can stop to think. In the theater, we can move our attention from one character or part of the stage to another. But in film and television, we see nothing at all except what the camera shows us.

Nonetheless, as in drama, we can discuss the nature of the scenery and other visual effects; as in drama and fiction, we can discuss the elements of conventional storytelling (character, plot, language); and as in fiction, we can discuss point of view—that is, how the camera is manipulated to achieve different effects. (To be sure, to do this last thing well requires a kind of technical knowledge entirely different from that required in the analysis of a play.) And at last, in writing about television and film, as in writing about any literary form, the most important element is the writer's clear awareness of his or her own responses, and his or her sensitivity to the artist behind the words and images. We must always be asking: *What does he get me to feel?* and *How does he get me to feel that way?* and *Why?*

CHAPTER 5

Literary Criticism and Theory

James Holstun

On December 10, 1513, the Renaissance humanist and political theorist Niccolò Machiavelli wrote a letter about life on his farm to his benefactor Francesco Vettori. Machiavelli says that, after amusing himself during the day with trivial pastimes, he returns home, doffs his day clothes, dons his "garments regal and courtly," and begins reading the works of Greek and Roman political writers:

> Reclothed appropriately, I enter the ancient courts of ancient men, where, received by them with affection, I feed on that food which only is mine and which I was born for, where I am not ashamed to speak with them and ask them the reason for their actions, and they in their kindness answer me; and for four hours of time I do not feel boredom, I forget every trouble, I do not dread poverty, I am not frightened by death; entirely I give myself over to them. (142)

This letter might mislead us into thinking of Machiavelli as a scholar-hermit; in fact, he was intimately involved in the turbulent political life

71

of his beloved Florence. But it does give us the striking image of a reader picturing his relation to the past as a textual conversation. As a result of this conversation with ancient authors, Machiavelli produced his *Discourses on Livy* and *The Prince,* two of the most important works of Renaissance political theory.

Renaissance humanists like Machiavelli built up a revolutionary model of reading as a conversation between men in time centering on concrete texts, argues historian J. G. A. Pocock in *The Machiavellian Moment.* True, medieval Scholastic philosophers also began with particular texts, but they often used them to discuss such abstract universals as being and essence. As a result, the text at hand might virtually disappear, but Renaissance humanists tried to preserve the concrete verbal quality of their texts, and so also their sense of a textual conversation with the past. This conversational reading led the humanists to conversational writing: to translations of classical literature into modern tongues, to a new literature modeling itself on these earlier texts, and to a new literary criticism that compared these Ancients and Moderns. Pocock also argues that the humanists' conversations with these texts of the past inspired them to begin thinking of their present-day social relations as a civil conversation about literature, political writing, and moral philosophy of the past and present (56–62).

□

Conversations—Critical and Theoretical

We literary critics could do worse than to define ourselves as the heirs of these humanist conversationalists—as readers in dialogue with texts of the past and with other readers (teachers, classmates, critics) who have also addressed them. Whether we are talking about Homer's *Odyssey,* George Eliot's *Middlemarch,* or last week's performance of *Waiting for Godot,* we come together around some text from the past and try to make sense of it in the present. We pose questions (silently, aloud, or in writing) of these texts and then articulate our answers. In this essay, I will speak of literary criticism as this sort of historical conversation with and about texts from the past. We might then think of the other chapters in this book as a series of conversational guidebooks—instructions in ways to make our conversations with these texts more sophisticated, pleasurable, and productive.

But what about "literary theory," the second part of my chapter title? The very term intimidates. If the model of literary criticism as textual conversation suggests a relaxed personal encounter, then "literary theory" suggests precisely the opposite: an impersonal, hard-edged, and rigorous approach to literature that cuts through the conversational niceties and gets down to science. Indeed, this model of literary theory has proved very attractive to twentieth-century literary critics. In a world increasingly dominated by technology, and in universities built around (and funded for) scientific research, literary critics have frequently found themselves trying to defend literary theory by presenting it as a rigorous, unified, quasi-scientific discipline.

If we listen more carefully to these claims for a unified, "scientific" theory, though, we'll hear an intriguing polyphony: many different critics claiming scientific authority for many different forms of literary theory, and getting into arguments with each other about which theory is truest to "the text itself." In other words, we discover spirited conversation about criticism, or (we might say more awkwardly) conversations about conversations about texts. Perhaps we can best define literary theory not as a logically unified science, but as a social institution: the sum of all these conversations and the settings (books, journals, departments of literature) that make them possible. When we "do literary theory," we are simply talking about the sorts of questions we should pose about literary texts, the sorts of conversations we should enter into about them. This chapter will examine some of the critical conversations (about literature) and theoretical conversations (about criticism) that twentieth-century literary critics have had. In the process, I hope it helps you become more aware of the literary theories you use and of alternative theories you might want to try on for size.

But you may very well object that you don't have a literary theory—that you just read the text itself and talk about what it means. This brings me to the most important point of this chapter: whether you know it or not, whether you like it or not, you already have at least an implicit theoretical point of view. Furthermore, the same is true of all your classmates, all your teachers, and all the writers in this book, for we all practice literary criticism by posing certain questions of literary texts and not others. A critic turning to *The Scarlet Letter* and asking, "What is the central imaginative unity of this work?" has already made at least one theoretical assumption: that criticism should discover and describe formal unities. A critic turning to the same work and asking, "How does Hawthorne present Hester's psychology as typical of women in general?" has made quite a different assumption: that criticism should examine literary models of gender identity. When these two critics start trying to justify beginning with one question and not the other, they are practicing literary theory. We study literary theory to make ourselves more conscious of the particular sorts of questions we pose (and do not pose) of texts, to discover new sorts of questions we might pose in the future, and to reflect on the social significance of our critical conversations.

One implication of all this is that when literary critics claim to be studying "the text itself," they are in fact studying it from a particular theoretical point of view they may not want (or be able) to articulate. In your career as an undergraduate critic, you may have heard someone say, "Now enough theory—let's look at the text itself!" We all probably feel that, when we interpret, we are interpreting the text itself, and the statement has the attractively commonsensical ring of a critic getting down to work. But if you listen harder, you may also hear some authoritarian overtones: the sound of critics squelching other sorts of questions and presenting theirs as the only ones possible. The next time someone tries to guide you toward "the text itself," listen carefully to the picture of "the text" that emerges from their discussion, and try to reconstruct their theoretical orientation—the particular sorts of questions they wish to pose and not to pose. If you happen to be in a classroom when you hear this claim and you are feeling particularly self-confident, try offering an alternative model of "the text itself"—say, by shifting the discussion of *The Scarlet Letter* from its imaginative unity to the disunity of gender roles it implies. You might note that, whereas suffering ennobles Hester Prynne, it destroys Arthur Dimmesdale, which could lead us to hypothesize that Hawthorne sees suffering as Woman's natural lot in life. With any luck, your instructor will entertain your question and the conversation will get more interesting.

Of course, you might not want to note any such thing—you might want to stick with and elaborate on the first theoretical position or move to some completely different one. And your instructor may swat you down, for critical conversations can be as one-sided and brutal as conversations of other sorts. But as soon as you begin comparing critical questions, you begin practicing literary theory. Literary theorists are simply literary critics who can discuss rationally why they pose certain sorts of critical questions and not others, without simply insisting that "the text itself" calls them forth.

□

Schools of Literary Theory

It's a little deceptive to refer to "schools" here. No particular sort of literary theory utterly dominates any literature department in any American university. Indeed, you'd have a hard time finding any theorist who would readily claim to be the devotee of any particular school, though as you might expect (since it's always more satisfying to classify than to be classified), theorists are more than willing to label each other. These schools contain internal factions; for instance, we frequently find psychoanalytic critics at each other's throats. And they interbreed gleefully, producing such hybrids as psychoanalytic deconstructionists and feminist Marxists. Nonetheless, some "school" labels help to get conversations going. I will not try to talk about all twentieth-century schools of literary theory, only about those you are still likely to encounter in some form in your courses and your reading. Under each heading, I will discuss first the origin and main premises of the school, then some of the main practitioners and their writings, then some of the places you are likely to encounter such theory at work, and finally some of the questions it typically poses of literary texts. I will not try to do a specific "reading" of any text from the point of view of each school, but you should certainly feel free to address these questions to any literary work you've read recently.

Old Historicism

This is a term I've cooked up to contrast with "New Criticism" and "New Historicism," which I will discuss later on. The old historicism was the sort of theory ruling American literary study until the end of World War II. It includes studies of philology and linguistics, source studies, and the history of ideas (which argues that literature expresses the intellectual history of its time in a rather straightforward fashion). For an example of the last, see E. M. W. Tillyard's *The Elizabethan World Picture,* which argues that Renaissance England was united by a single, hierarchical world picture that we can see represented in a number of different works. Meyer H. Abrams's *The Mirror and the Lamp,* though informed by New Critical methods of close reading, does something similar for the world view of the Romantic era. We might also group with the old historicism the sort of literary biography that sees literature as the straightforward expression of the author's personality.

This sort of history of ideas or intellectual history approach is an essential component of all literary criticism. You may well encounter it in survey courses that try to cover long epochs (*"Beowulf* to Burns"), in the introductory essays that preface scholarly editions of literary works, and (to some extent) in the lectures and criticism of all critics, even those New Critics who profess to despise appeals to extraliterary influences.

TYPICAL QUESTIONS

What were the literary influences on this work, and what works did it influence in turn?

How does this work reflect the world view of its time or the social milieu of the writer?

How does it reflect its author's personality and opinions?

The New Criticism

Forty years old, but still alive and kicking, the New Criticism is the single most powerful movement in twentieth-century American literary criticism. Because of this, and because later literary theories defined themselves in part as reactions to the New Criticism, it deserves a fairly long consideration here. From the first, the New Criticism was not just an esoteric theory, but a pedagogical method. After World War II, when American colleges admitted more and more men (and later, women), New Criticism provided the country's swelling English classes with an analytical method and a program. It attacked the old historicism, arguing that we should set aside such questions as the work's relation to society, its effect on audiences, and the author's biography and intentions, and focus on "intrinsic" criticism of "the work itself."

The New Criticism claims to be a science of literature, one that need not enter into conversation with such "extrinsic" disciplines as psychology, philosophy, history, or economics. It argues that we can reach the clearest possible understanding of the literary artifact by concentrating on its patterns of sound, metaphors, and narrative structure. The New Criticism found lyric poetry most amenable to its sort of structural analysis. When it turned to works in other genres, even the most diffuse and rambling novel, it labored to discover or construct the essential "poetic" forms unifying them; if it couldn't, it tended to dismiss them as substandard.

To its credit, the New Criticism frequently smuggled in the back door those critical questions it shoved out the front, and if we read the New Criticism carefully, we can find more or less covert analyses of authorial intention, audience response, and literary sociology and history. But these analyses tend almost invariably in the direction of *unity*. They give us an image of authors out to crystallize their noncontradictory intentions in unified literary artifacts, a community of readers contemplating these artifacts in unison, and a literary history consisting of an assembly of elegantly crafted literary mechanisms. Because it insisted so stridently that this model of literary culture was a product of the work itself, it attempted to shunt aside theories that might question its conclusions.

Still, it is too easy to dismiss the New Criticism as dogmatic formalism and to ignore its remarkable power for putting students quickly into conversation with a certain model of their literary heritage. We could even argue that there is a democratic and populist current at work in the New Criticism, since it claims to show students how to master certain techniques of close reading (the analysis of connotation, metaphor, irony, plot, point of view) and become their own authorities. In this sense, the chapters in this book on poetry, drama, and fiction are New Critical.

Some of the more important New Critical works are Cleanth Brooks's *The Well Wrought Urn,* John Crowe Ransom's *The World's Body,* René Wellek and Austin Warren's *The Theory of Literature,* and William K. Wimsatt and Monroe C. Beardsley's *The Verbal Icon.* For histories, see Murray Krieger's *The New Apologists for Poetry* for a look from the inside, and John Fekete's *The Critical Twilight* for a look from the outside.

Until 1960 or so, the New Criticism held almost unchallenged power in American departments of literature, which meant that "the text itself" became a synonym for "the text as defined by the New Criticism." Most of your professors were probably trained in the New Criticism, though they may later have moved away from it. But when you hear them arguing that a poem, play, or novel is an artifact structurally unified by its own irony, poetic texture, or verbal complexity, then the chances are good that you are hearing at least an echo of the New Criticism. You are more likely to hear the New Criticism in introductory literature courses that emphasize skills of close reading, even when your professor is a Marxist, feminist, or deconstructionist who has serious disagreements with the New Criticism as a theoretical approach. Even though the New Criticism is in decline (few people would now identify themselves with it), its influence is everywhere. You will encounter it at work in practically every piece of literary criticism published in this country between 1950 and 1970. Collections of critical essays and casebooks (such as the Norton Critical Editions), which target a large, conservatively defined market, tend to have editors who choose New Critical essays.

TYPICAL QUESTIONS

What is the unifying structure of this work?

How does its form reflect its content?

How do its verbal texture and its imagery enhance its logical structure?

How does it achieve a harmony between opposing principles, and shut out the chaotic intrusions of the extraliterary world?

Psychoanalytic Criticism

We can best mark the decline of American New Criticism by the 1957 publication of *The Anatomy of Criticism,* by the Canadian critic Northrop Frye. Frye argues that the entirety of literature (not just the individual work) forms a unified system, a system defined not just by its own sense of structure, but by the way it gives shape to human desire. Though Frye's work is not typically classified as psychoanalytic criticism, we might usefully compare it to the work of the Swiss psychologist Carl Gustav Jung. As Jung argues that archetypal aspects of the collective unconscious determine individual psychology, Frye argues that certain literary archetypes determine the structure and function of individual literary works. Though much criticized and little imitated, *The Anatomy of Criticism* remains a towering achievement of modern literary theory. After its publication, American literary theory never again achieved the sort of consensus it did during the heyday of the New Criticism. It began to hybridize with a number of "extrinsic" disciplines (frequently European in origin), such as Freudian psychoanalysis, structuralism, and Marxism. Now the conversations get louder and more boisterous.

Freudian psychoanalytic criticism is an example of that biographical or "intentionalist" criticism for which the New Criticism has such a profound distrust. It works against the New Criticism by arguing that unresolved and sometimes unconscious ambivalences in the author's own life may lead to a disunified (but not for that reason esthetically inferior) literary work. It aims to show that literature is always structured by complex and contradictory human desires, not just by an ideal of formal unity. Psychoanalytic critics typically argue that the very narrative structure of a novel or autobiography is a sublimated (repressed, recoded, and expressed) version of some underlying psychological force or event.

Some psychoanalytic critics attempt to read an author's own family life and traumas in the actions of their characters. And some proponents of a dogmatic Freudianism claim a universal truth for Freud's model of the Oedipus complex, claiming that it explains all literature from Sophocles to Virginia Woolf. But others (notably Freudo-Marxists and Freudo-feminists) claim that Freudian psychoanalysis works best as a tool for examining the nineteenth- and twentieth-century bourgeois family that Freud himself was familiar with, and for analyzing authors who grew up in and portray such families. More recent structuralist models of psychoanalytic criticism argue that language is not merely the literary medium through which we perceive human desire, but the very substance and object of that desire.

Freud's writings are full of literary criticism: analyses of Greek drama, folktales, the Hebrew Scriptures, and German fiction. See particularly his *The Interpretation of Dreams* and *The Uncanny.* See also Shoshona Felman's *Writing and Madness,* Norman N. Holland's *The Dynamics of Literary Response,* Ernest Jones's *Hamlet and His Problems,* and Jacques Lacan's *Ecrits.*

Departments of literature don't look down on psychoanalytic criticism as much as they once did. Indeed, psychoanalysis has shown a remarkable capacity for hybridizing, and one can encounter psychoanalytic versions of every school in this list from the New Criticism on. It's everywhere. As with Marxist literary criticism, one can find strong critiques of one psychoanalytical critical position coming from another. A fierce controversy rages, for instance, between orthodox Freudian and feminist psychoanalytical critics.

TYPICAL QUESTIONS

How does this work dramatize the author's unresolved childhood conflicts?

How does it reveal the particular psychological dilemmas and conflicts produced by family life during a particular historical period?

What is the connection between the desires of the characters *in* the work, the desire of the author in *writing* the work, and the desire of the reader in *reading* the work? In other words, what is the connection between literary language and desire?

Reader Response Criticism

As psychoanalytic criticism violates the New Critical taboo against inquiring after the author's psychology and intention, so reader response criticism violates the New Critical taboo against inquiring after the work's effects on its readers. It sees the literary work not as a sort of object existing in space independently of its readers, but as the temporal experience of a reader or a community of readers. Reader response criticism is not a terribly impressionistic sort of criticism—the unfocused musings of this reader or that. It exceeds even the formal rigor of the New Criticism by analyzing the specific effects of particular passages in a novel or lines in a poem. Nor is it a criticism aimed strictly at individual literary responses; indeed, many reader response critics do a sort of literary sociology by focusing on the modes of reading and interpreting employed by entire communities of readers. But it does move away from the New Critical "work itself" to the interpretive conventions that help define what that work means to readers. Reader response critics frequently argue that different communities of readers may bring such radically different interpretive conventions to bear that they may pick up the same text and literally find themselves reading different books.

See Umberto Eco's *The Role of the Reader,* Judith Fetterly's *The Resisting Reader,* Stanley Fish's *Self-Consuming Artifacts,* Wolfgang Iser's *The Implied Reader,* and *Reader-Response Criticism,* edited by Jane P. Tompkins.

Like psychoanalytic criticism, reader response criticism has thrived and made itself at home in the post–New Critical department of literature, and you will encounter it in many different classes and literary journals. We might think of it as an attempt to extend drama criticism to nondramatic genres, for it insists that all literature is a structure of experience, not just a form or meaning. You may first encounter a sort of reader (or "audience") response criticism in drama classes; James Howe's chapter on drama in this book, for instance, practices a version of reader/audience response criticism.

TYPICAL QUESTIONS

How does the reader join with the author to help the text mean?

What is the significance of the series of interpretations the reader goes through in the process of reading?

What sort of reader and what community of readers does this work imply and help to create?

Structuralism and Deconstruction

Structuralism derives from a variety of sources, including Marx, Freud, the Swiss linguist Ferdinand de Saussure, the French anthropologist Claude Lévi-Strauss, and the Polish linguist Roman Jakobson. Structuralism claims that human culture itself is fundamentally a language, a complex system of signifieds (concepts) and signifiers. These signifiers can be verbal (like language itself or literature) or nonverbal (like face painting, advertising, or fashion). Because it sees all culture as a language, structuralism can apply structural linguistics to a wide variety of disciplines: anthropology, psychoanalysis, history, political theory, and literary criticism.

In literary studies, structuralism has had two divergent effects. First, it has produced a quasi-scientific formalism analyzing the intrinsic structure of the literary work with a rigor far surpassing even that of the New Criticism. See, for instance, Roland Barthes' *S/Z,* which breaks down a Zola novella into a complex structure of literary "codes." Second, it has been a powerful tool of ideological analysis showing the extraordinary linguistic richness of both the literary and the extraliterary worlds. See, for instance, Barthes' *Mythologies,* which examines the mass culture of the capitalist West as an oppressive language that gives its consumers a delusive, mythic "knowledge" of the world. These effects may seem to be at odds, and they frequently are. But they need not be: as Barthes himself has said, "A little formalism leads one away from history; a lot leads one back again" (*Mythologies* 112).

The French philosopher Jacques Derrida has criticized and developed structuralist analysis, producing the philosophical and literary theory known as "poststructuralism" or "deconstruction," which takes as its opponent what it calls "the metaphysics of presence." This is the claim of literature or philosophy that we can find some full, rich meaning outside of or prior to language itself. Deconstruction claims that the metaphysics of presence rests on certain binary oppositions which cannot ultimately be maintained—for example, oppositions between presence and absence, nature and culture, speech and writing. From a deconstructive perspective, the New Critical distinction between "extrinsic" and "intrinsic" criticism is one such foredoomed and metaphysical opposition: no literary work can be analyzed "intrinsically," for by its very nature, it implies the entire "extrinsic" world of language. Deconstructive criticism typically argues that a particular literary, historical, or philosophical work both claims to possess full and immediate presence and admits the impossibility of attaining such presence. As interpreted and popularized by the Yale School of literary criticism (Paul de Man, Geoffrey Hartman, J. Hillis Miller, and on the periphery, Harold Bloom), deconstruction has come to be a substantial force in American literary criticism.

See Jonathan Culler's *Structuralist Poetics,* Paul de Man's *Allegories of Reading,* Jacques Derrida's *Of Grammatology* and *Positions,* Ferdinand de Saussure's *Course in General Linguistics,* Claude Lévi-Strauss's *Structural Anthropology,* and *The Structuralist Controversy,* edited by Richard Macksey and Eugenio Donato.

No literary theory raises conservative critical hackles more quickly than deconstruction, which is probably the most actively debated literary theory of the 1980s. Yet it seems to have settled rather easily into departments of literature, and you may frequently hear deconstructionist terminology coming from professors you thought were dyed-in-the-wool New Critics. Deconstruction does attack New Critical claims for the unified presence of the literary work, but it too tends to limit itself to canonical literary works, so it slips easily into preestablished literary curricula. The familiar canon reappears in deconstructionist guise as that group of works *most aware of* the impossibility of maintaining pure literary presence.

TYPICAL QUESTIONS

What is the linguistic structure of this literary work?

How does this structure tie it to anthropology, psychology, and extraliterary reality more generally?

How does its narrative structure show it to be an ideological or cultural project?

How do its claims to authenticity and self-presence undercut or deconstruct themselves?

Differential Criticism

This is another made up "school name," one that groups together the study of literature by and about oppressed groups, including ethnics, women, and gays. Where the old historicism and the New Criticism looked for formal unities and literary traditions, differential criticism looks for cultural difference. Differential critics might turn to "the American tradition in literature" and find repressed literatures by and about one people almost exterminated by the European settlements of America (Native Americans) and another who participated in that settlement unwillingly (Afro-Americans). Or they might look at "the Western tradition in literature" (a tradition much celebrated by T. S. Eliot and conservative pedagogues such as William Bennett) and find that this tradition has defined itself partly by stifling the voices of women and by demonizing (among others) Jews and Muslims. One of the most important (and most radical arguments) of differential criticism is that margins are, in fact, at the center—that the most conservative and canonical writers are preoccupied with cultural difference. For instance, historicist feminists have examined considerations of gender difference by Chaucer, Shakespeare, and Milton. In *Such Is My Love,* Joseph Pequigney shows that the language of gay love pervades Shakespeare's *Sonnets.*

See Henry Louis Gates' *Black Literature and Literary Theory* and (ed.) *"Race," Writing, and Difference,* Sandra Gilbert and Susan Gubar's *Madwoman in the Attic,* Edward Said's *Orientalism,* and *Making a Difference,* edited by Gayle Greene and Coppélia Kahn. There are entire journals of differential cultural study: *Feminist Studies* and *Signs* for feminism and lesbianism, *The Journal of Homosexuality* for gays, and *Eire Ireland,* Black Literature Forum, and many others for particular ethnic traditions.

Differential criticism entered American literature departments during the 1960s and 1970s as an academic branch of the black, women's, and gay liberation movements. At first, it was marginalized in special programs and courses (Black Studies programs, "Women Novelists of the Nineteenth Century"), and one is still less likely to hear (for example) a man professing feminist criticism than a woman. But most literature departments and journals are opening up to differential criticism. Even some of the more conservative anthologies are making an effort to incorporate more authors (sometimes even editors) who are not straight white males.

TYPICAL QUESTIONS

How has the literary tradition constructed models of identity for oppressed groups?

How has the literary canon excluded the work of writers who belong to these groups?

How have these groups constructed oppositional literary identities for themselves?

How might different communities of readers interpret the same text differently?

Michel Foucault and the New Historicism

The distance we have traveled from the New Critics' attempt to fabricate a specifically literary critical science is apparent in the growing influence of Michel Foucault, a French historian and philosopher who typically studied not literature, but social institutions such as psychoanalysis, the asylum, and the prison. Foucault's work centers on the ways in which Western culture has used discipline to create models of human identity, and the ways in which human subjects have fashioned identities for themselves. Foucault's work has entered into American literary criticism through the culture criticism of Edward Said and through the work of a loosely knit group of historians, anthropologists, and literary critics known as the new historicists. They draw on psychoanalysis, feminism, and deconstruction, but primarily on Foucault, to show the political function of literature and the symbolic structuring of extraliterary reality. They concern themselves with the concept of *power*, the complex means by which societies produce and reproduce themselves. Where the old historicism might look to Shakespeare's plays to see a unified and hierarchical Elizabethan world picture, the new historicism might look to see how they reveal the symbolic structure of Renaissance conflicts over race, class, and gender.

See Nancy Armstrong's *Desire and Domestic Fiction,* Foucault's *The Foucault Reader,* Stephen Greenblatt's *Renaissance Self-Fashioning,* Said's *The World, the Text, and the Critic,* and the journal *Representations.*

The New Historicism is primarily a phenomenon of the 1980s, and you are more likely to hear New Historicist arguments from younger academics. All the same, it has already produced an impressive body of literary scholarship. Like American deconstruction, it has fared better in departments of literature than one might have expected, in part because of the supple power of its analyses, in part because it too takes pains to distinguish itself from most sorts of Marxist criticism—the hoary bugaboo of American literary studies.

Typical Questions

What does this work reveal about the connections between language, knowledge, and power in a particular culture?

What model of human personality, what image of the human body, does this work imply or construct?

How does this work reveal a historically specific model of truth and authority?

Marxist Literary Criticism

Some of my students have been surprised to find that there is such a thing as Marxist literary criticism, thinking that Marxists must have better things to do (economic analysis, class struggle) than analyze literature. But some of the most important twentieth-century developments in Marxist thought have been in the realm of cultural studies, and we find Marxist analyses of literary genres that might not seem at first to lend themselves to social criticism. For instance, the German Marxist Walter Benjamin wrote a brilliant study entitled *Charles Baudelaire: A Lyric Poet in the Era of High*

Capitalism in which he reconstructs the social resonances of Baudelaire's romantic and estheticist verse.

Marxism argues that human history is a series of struggles between oppressed and oppressing classes; Marxist literary criticism argues that literature always participates in this struggle. Like the New Historicism, it resists the unifying impulse of the old historicism and the New Criticism by arguing for strong connections between a literary work and the contradictory relations among classes when it was written. It argues both that literature reflects social institutions and that it is itself an important social institution in its own right, with a particular ideological function.

One of the most impressive works of Marxist literary criticism is Fredric Jameson's *The Political Unconscious: Narrative as a Socially Symbolic Act*, which synthesizes the work of structuralists and poststructuralists, European Marxists, and North American literary critics to create a powerful analysis of the work done by narrative, primarily nineteenth- and twentieth-century novels. In an earlier work, *Marxism and Form*, Jameson did much to introduce American literary critics to the cultural theory of European Marxists. See also Theodor W. Adorno's *Prisms*, Benjamin's *Illuminations*, Georg Lukács's *Writer and Critic*, Pierre Machery's *A Theory of Literary Production*, Raymond Williams's *Marxism and Literature*, and the journals *New Left Review*, *Social Text*, and *Telos*.

It is not altogether a coincidence that American New Criticism rose at the same time as McCarthyism. As McCarthyism tried to protect "American values" from an "external" Marxist threat (including Marxist academics), so the New Criticism tried to protect "the literary work itself" from "extrinsic" modes of literary criticism (including Marxist literary criticism). And most American literary critics still work hard to deny or recode Marxist influences on their work. But if you hear discussions of literary ideology, or of class and form, genre, autobiography, narrative, and so on, then you are probably hearing Marxist theory at work.

Typical Questions

How does this literary work reflect the author's class, or the author's analysis of class relations?

What is the relation in this work between class and such literary matters as genre, narrative, style, characterization?

What is this work's *ideological* vision—how does it attempt to shore up an oppressive social order and idealize social conflicts out of existence?

What is this work's *utopian* vision—what alternative collective life does it propose as a solution to these conflicts?

How can we break down the institutional barriers between Marxist literary theory and other forms of revolutionary cultural practice?

□

How to Begin Doing Literary Theory

As I've argued, you are already possessed of (or by) a literary theory that governs your conversations with texts and with other critics. But if you wish to become more self-conscious about your theory and enter directly into theoretical conversations about critical approaches, several possible routes lie before you.

In her chapter on the critical essay, Robyn Warhol recommends that you begin writing a critical essay not with secondary research, but with some personal interest in and thesis about a literary work. This is just as true for studying literary theory: it is far too complex to begin studying all at once. Literary theory gives bookstore organizers the shakes, for it lurches and dribbles off into history, philosophy, anthropology, political science, and linguistics with no warning. This is part of its protean appeal. But if you try to swallow it whole, it will eat you alive. Rather than trying to tame this seething brute all at once, begin with some concrete problem you're interested in: the peculiar structure of Shakespeare's romances, the relation between pictorial and verbal art in Blake's prints, the idea of gay identity in modern American fiction. Then ask your instructor what different theoretical approaches critics have taken to these works, and what additional readings might be helpful—for these examples, general studies of the nature of genre, of pictorial-verbal relations, and of gender identity. Find these works, read them, and compare them. Then you will be off and running—in dialogue with criticism and theories other than your own, and no doubt alerted to additional works you will read soon. If your instructor hears the word "theory," turns pale and frothy, and starts shouting about "the text itself," just ask what depraved persons in your department have been known to commit theory and go talk to them.

You could also begin by reading a guidebook to literary theory—a subtler and more thorough version of my list of theoretical schools above. René Wellek and Austin Warren's New Critical manifesto, *Theory of Literature,* is thirty-eight years old, as of my writing, but it is still a learned and provocative study. Terry Eagleton's *Literary Theory: An Introduction* is a good guide to recent theory because of its readable and colloquial style, its helpful bibliography, and its explicitly Marxist theoretical stance; Eagleton wastes no time claiming to be a neutral, scientific voice of reason, so you will find it easy to enter into a spirited conversation with him right away. If you have time, it might be interesting to compare Eagleton with Wellek and Warren to get a sense of the conversations Marxists and New Critics have with each other. For instance, Wellek and Warren call Marxists "irrationalists," and Eagleton says the same of New Critics.

Alternatively, you might want to survey some of the primary sources. Taken together, Hazard Adams's anthology *Critical Theory Since Plato* and Adams and Leroy Searle's *Critical Theory Since 1965* form a massive and comprehensive anthology of theoretical statements. Or look at one of the special topics anthologies I mention in my discussion of "schools." Or simply browse through one of the modern journals of literary theory and cultural criticism that encourage diverse critical viewpoints: *Critical Inquiry, Diacritics, ELH, The Minnesota Review, New Literary History, PMLA, Representations, Signs, Social Text,* and many others.

Or you might just want to pick some major theoretical text and plunge in—reading slowly and carefully and taking careful, critical notes. I began my undergraduate study of literary theory by immersing myself in Northrop Frye's *Anatomy of Criticism.* Since literary theory is a conversation, not a logical structure, you can get a good sense of the whole terrain by looking at it from one theorist's polemical point of view.

□

Some Implications

We should now turn to some of the implications for your own writing of this conversational model of criticism and theory. The alternative critical interpretations and theoretical methods you encounter will probably be those of your instructor and the critics you read when researching your topic. If you wish to keep your conversations lively, honest, and open to response by others, you must confront several ethical questions. First, when writing on works your instructors have already spoken on, you must define your theoretical stance in relation to theirs. This is not easy. As you think more and more about literary theory, you will have a clearer sense of your instructors' stances, but you will be left with a problem: are they willing to engage you in critical debate? Many instructors will practically insist on it, but if you run into any who want you to paraphrase their arguments, then you must decide whether to give in or to rebel. One compromise is to take your instructor's theoretical stance and basic reading of a work and extend it to other works or to other parts of the work they haven't talked about. While this approach will not help you broaden your theoretical perspectives much, it will help you avoid losing your identity altogether.

You face a slightly different situation when you begin a conversation with the writings of some other critic. A frequent undergraduate encounter with literary criticism goes something like this: the day before the paper is due, you rush frantically through the library stacks trying to find that one book or article that will "give you some ideas" for the paper. If you are lucky enough to find it (and some unnaturally early riser from your class will typically have checked it out scant minutes before your arrival), lack of time will keep you from having a genuine theoretical conversation, forcing you into one of three unsavory alternatives.

Plagiarism

This is the critical-conversational equivalent of a ventriloquist's act, with you as the dummy. Plagiarism destroys critical conversation, since you're not talking with anyone about a shared literary text, but transcribing someone else's conversation. And it destroys theoretical conversation, because you don't even begin to examine your critic's theoretical assumptions or to articulate your own. In an act of critical self-extinction, you sign away all your rights to a voice of your own and produce a somewhat garbled version of someone else's voice. The Latin root of *plagiarist* is *plagiarus* or "kidnapper," but oddly enough, it's you who's being kidnapped, taken over by the voice of your critical victim/victimizer.

Paraphrase

Here, you simply repeat someone else's argument in your own words, but acknowledge your intellectual debt. This may be ethically preferable to red-handed plagiarism, but it leaves your critical and theoretical conversation just as barren. You lose your identity and sing harmony to some presumed authority voice. Of course, some paraphrase is essential for any critical paper incorporating secondary research, but make sure your own voice predominates. Three hints. First, write out the main idea of each paragraph in the body of your paper. If this idea isn't yours but some other critic's, then begin developing your argument. This isn't an absolute rule (I break it myself in the first two paragraphs of this chapter), but long passages of paraphrase can stifle your critical voice, particularly if they come in the middle of your paper (where you should be developing your own position), or at the conclusion (where you should be driving it home). Second, check your footnotes or running annotations. Take more than a few references to the same source as a danger signal, particularly if they all come in a row. Third, try to begin and end each paragraph with your own voice, not with a quotation or paraphrase of someone else's. Again, this is by no means a hard and fast rule. But paragraph beginnings and endings are power points, and you risk losing control of the conversation if you let other critics take over there.

Source Mining

Here, you simply go digging through your critical sources to accumulate opinion nuggets similar to your own. This is a critical conversation of sorts, but a pretty tedious one: "I think color symbolism is important in *The Scarlet Letter,* and so do critics A, B, and C." Such an argument reveals a critical intelligence ill at ease with itself, neither secure about the opinions it does hold nor bold enough to push on to some new opinion. Ask yourself, "What are the theoretical assumptions motivating this obnoxiously repetitive emphasis on color symbolism in literature?" then say something new that distinguishes you from this repetitious trio of critical dullards.

However, if you've followed Richard Sweterlitsch's advice in "Doing Literary Research" and Robyn Warhol's "Writing the Critical Essay," then you have time to conduct a genuine theoretical conversation by reading carefully through the critics you've chosen to speak with, noting their points of agreement and disagreement, formulating the theoretical assumptions underlying their critical claims, and (most important) discovering the opportunities for your original critical perspective. You have time to engage in a critical conversation of genuine interest to you and your readers.

□

Afterwords

Three parting thoughts. First, I have argued that we can never begin doing criticism without some theoretical assumptions, but there is or should be a flip side to this claim: we should never finish doing criticism without reexamining and modifying, however slightly, our theoretical assumptions. Few spectacles are more depressing than the sight of some unreflective critic hacking at some new literary work with the same old unmodified theoretical tools: "Theory A once again reveals its ineluctable analytical force—now where's my next victim?" Part of the pleasure of doing theory is the pleasure of self-examination—of seeing how your theoretical assumptions change in the course of critical practice. For instance, when you feel your deconstructionist theory blunting itself against "Daisy Miller," you may find yourself turning for help to feminism, perhaps forging a deconstructive feminism in the process. The power of theory is not its hard-edged certainty, but its malleability.

Second: One might expect that the way a theorist outlines contemporary schools of literary theory would reveal something about that theorist's own theory. One might expect, for instance, that they would be unlikely to begin the list with the sort they practice, but quite likely to conclude with that sort. And in fact, that is the case with the series I've constructed, for it concludes with differential criticism, the New Historicism, and Marxism, the schools I am currently most interested in. This chapter reflects my own theoretical interests and assumptions in myriad ways (many of which I am no doubt ignorant of). But this is as it must be: just as there is no neutral criticism of "the text itself," so there is no neutral presentation of literary theories.

Third: a return to the conversational leitmotif of this chapter. If you compare my list of theoretical schools with that shorter but similar list constructed by my colleague Robyn Warhol, you will notice that we characterize some critical schools differently and even fabricate completely different ones. Did somebody get it wrong? Did we fail to read each other's chapters? Not really. Her listing reflects her perception of the contemporary state of literary theory as mine reflects mine. Our differences indicate a genuine theoretical difference of opinion—one that has led to some interesting conversations in the past, and which I'm sure will lead to more in the future. But that's the nature of theory—to be loquacious. If you want to get in on the conversation, then start talking back.

□

Works Cited

Abrams, Meyer H. *The Mirror and the Lamp: Romantic Theory and the Critical Tradition.* New York: Oxford UP, 1953.

Adams, Hazard, ed. *Critical Theory Since Plato.* New York: Harcourt, 1971.

Adams, Hazard, and Leroy Searle. *Critical Theory Since 1965.* Tallahassee: U Presses of Florida, Florida State UP, 1986.

Adorno, Theodor W. *Prisms.* Trans. Samuel Weber and Shierry Weber. London: Neville Spearman, 1967.

Armstrong, Nancy. *Desire and Domestic Fiction.* New York: Oxford UP, 1987.

Barthes, Roland. *Mythologies.* Trans. Annette Lavers. New York: Hill and Wang, 1972.

———. *S/Z.* Trans. Richard Miller. New York: Hill and Wang, 1974.

Benjamin, Walter: *Charles Baudelaire: A Lyric Poet in the Era of High Capitalism.* London: New Left Books, 1973.

———. *Illuminations.* Ed. Hannah Arendt. Trans. Harry Zohn. New York: Schocken, 1977.

Brooks, Cleanth. *The Well-Wrought Urn: Studies in the Structure of Poetry.* New York: Harcourt, 1947.

Culler, Jonathan. *Structuralist Poetics: Structuralism, Linguistics, and the Study of Language.* Ithaca: Cornell UP, 1975.

de Man, Paul. *Allegories of Reading: Figural Language in Rousseau, Nietzsche, Rilke, and Proust.* New Haven: Yale UP, 1979.

Derrida, Jacques. *Of Grammatology.* Trans. Gayatri Spivak. Baltimore: Johns Hopkins UP, 1976.

———. *Positions.* Trans. Alan Bass. Chicago: U of Chicago P, 1981.

Eagleton, Terry. *Literary Theory: An Introduction.* Minneapolis: U of Minnesota P, 1983.

Eco, Umberto. *The Role of the Reader: Explorations in the Semiotics of Texts.* Bloomington: Indiana UP, 1979.

Fekete, John. *The Critical Twilight: Explorations in the Ideology of Anglo-American Literary Theory from Eliot to McLuhan.* London and Boston: Routledge, 1977.

Felman, Shoshona. *Writing and Madness (Literature/Philosophy/Psychoanalysis).* Trans. Martha Noel Evans and the author. Ithaca: Cornell UP, 1985.

Fetterly, Judith. *The Resisting Reader: A Feminist Approach to American Fiction.* Bloomington: Indiana UP, 1978.

Fish, Stanley. *Self-Consuming Artifacts: The Experience of Seventeenth-Century Literature.* Berkeley and Los Angeles: U of California P, 1972.

Foucault, Michel. *The Foucault Reader.* Ed. Paul Rabinow. New York: Pantheon, 1984.

Freud, Sigmund. *The Interpretation of Dreams.* Trans. James Strachey. New York: Avon, 1965.

———. *On "The Uncanny".* James Strachey, ed. *The Standard Edition of the Complete Psychological Works of Sigmund Freud: Volume XVII (1917–1919), An Infantile Neurosis and Other Works.* London: Hogarth P and the Institute of Psycho-Analysis, 1955, 217–52.

Frye, Northrop. *The Anatomy of Criticism: Four Essays.* Princeton: Princeton UP, 1957.

Gates, Henry Louis. *Black Literature and Literary Theory.* London and New York: Methuen, 1984.

———, ed. *"Race," Writing, and Difference.* Chicago: U of Chicago P, 1986.

Gilbert, Sandra, and Susan Gubar. *The Madwoman in the Attic: The Woman Writer and the Nineteenth-Century Literary Imagination.* New Haven: Yale UP, 1979.

Greenblatt, Stephen. *Renaissance Self-Fashioning: From More to Shakespeare.* Chicago: U of Chicago P, 1980.

Greene, Gayle, and Coppélia Kahn, eds. *Making a Difference: Feminist Literary Criticism.* London and New York: Methuen, 1985.

Holland, Norman N. *The Dynamics of Literary Response.* New York: Oxford UP, 1968.

Iser, Wolfgang. *The Implied Reader: Patterns of Communication in Prose Fiction from Bunyan to Beckett.* Baltimore: Johns Hopkins UP, 1974.

Jameson, Fredric. *Marxism and Form: Twentieth-Century Dialectical Theories of Literature.* Princeton: Princeton UP, 1971.

———. *The Political Unconscious: Narrative as a Socially Symbolic Act.* Ithaca: Cornell UP, 1981.

Jones, Ernest. *Hamlet and Oedipus.* Garden City: Doubleday, 1949.

Krieger, Murray. *The New Apologists for Poetry.* Minneapolis: U of Minnesota P, 1956.

Lacan, Jacques. *Ecrits.* Trans. Alan Sheridan. New York: Norton, 1977.

Lévi-Strauss, Claude. *Structural Anthropology.* Trans. Claire Jacobson and Brooke Grundfest Schoepf. New York: Basic, 1963.

Lukács, Georg. *Writer and Critic and Other Essays.* New York: Grosset, 1970.

Machery, Pierre. *A Theory of Literary Production.* Trans. Geoffrey Wall. London: Routledge, 1978.

Machiavelli, Niccolò. *The Letters of Machiavelli: A Selection of His Letters.* Trans. and ed. Allan Gilbert. New York: Capricorn, 1961.

Macksey, Richard, and Eugenio Donato. *The Languages of Criticism and the Sciences of Man: The Structuralist Controversy.* Baltimore: Johns Hopkins UP, 1970.

Pequigney, Joseph. *Such is My Love: A Study of Shakespeare's Sonnets.* Chicago: U of Chicago P, 1985.

Pocock, J. G. A. *The Machiavellian Moment: Florentine Political Thought and the Atlantic Republican Tradition.* Princeton: Princeton UP, 1975.

Ransom, John Crowe. *The World's Body.* Baton Rouge: Louisiana State UP, 1968.

Said, Edward. *Orientalism.* New York: Pantheon, 1978.

———. *The World, the Text, and the Critic.* Cambridge: Harvard UP, 1983.

Saussure, Ferdinand de. *Course in General Linguistics.* New York: McGraw-Hill, 1959.

Tillyard, E. M. W. *The Elizabethan World Picture.* New York: Vintage, n.d.

Tompkins, Jane P., ed. *Reader-Response Criticism: From Formalism to Post-Structuralism.* Baltimore: Johns Hopkins UP, 1980.

Wellek, René, and Austin Warren. *The Theory of Literature.* 3rd ed. New York: Harcourt, 1977.

Williams, Raymond. *Marxism and Literature.* Oxford: Oxford UP, 1977.

Wimsatt, William K., and Monroe C. Beardsley. *The Verbal Icon: Studies in the Meaning of Poetry.* Louisville: U of Kentucky P, 1954.

PART TWO

□

Writing as a
Reader

□

CHAPTER 6

Writing Critical Essays

Robyn Warhol

W hen literature professors assign you to "write a paper," what exactly do they want you to do? Some instructors are precise about assignments: they may specify a topic or even a thesis; they may supply the evidence on which you are to comment. Often, though—especially in more advanced English courses—the assignment is "open." What, then, is your professor looking for?

Probably he or she expects you to write a "critical essay," a relatively brief paper in which you will apply your ingenuity, creativity, and analytical skills to confronting and explaining a literary text. A paper qualifies as a critical essay when it makes an original observation about a work of literature while answering the question, "Well, so what?"

You may find yourself a bit overcome at the prospect of coming up with something original to say about a work by Chaucer, Shakespeare, Austen, or Faulkner: haven't professional scholars been writing everything that could possibly be said, for decades if not for centuries? Intimidated by this assumption, many students go to the library and look up what "the critics" have said before trying to work on criticism of their own. I don't think that's a good way to go about it. Even if you are assigned to write a research paper (which differs from a critical essay in that it requires you to consult and cite other scholars' work), you will find the writing less difficult if you work out your own critical position on a text before consulting other sources. You can always revise your ideas and your essay as your understanding of the text increases. For this, after all, is the purpose of writing critical essays: to come to a more complete understanding of a given work of literature and to communicate that understanding to another reader.

☐

What Critical Essays Do

"Critical," in literary matters, does not carry the negative connotations of "finding fault" that the word has in common usage. Most critical essays either imply or express a great deal of enthusiasm for the works they discuss. The reason is simple: it's much more productive to spend time thinking and writing about a poem, play, story, or novel you enjoyed reading than to dwell on one you didn't like in the first place. Devoting the necessary hours to tearing apart a work you found boring or offensive or amateurish can be depressing.

In literary study, critical essays usually have one of three main goals. They can aim primarily to *describe, evaluate,* or *interpret* a text. All essays will combine some elements of each activity. For instance, "evaluation" is implicit in every critical essay. Even if you don't set out to prove how good a particular text is, you imply that it has value when you choose it as the subject for critical study. Still, every essay's main point, or *thesis,* should focus on one of these three main questions: How does this text work? Is this text any good? What does this text mean?

The Descriptive Critical Essay

When you write a descriptive critical essay, the main question you are trying to answer is: How does this literary text work? How does it get its meaning across? The broad term for this kind of study is "poetics" or—as Jonathan Culler has defined it—the study of the codes and conventions, the recurring patterns and familiar structures, that make it possible for literary texts to have "meaning" (37). In student writing, the descriptive critical essay usually focuses on specific features of one text, and sometimes compares a given text to a model of the genre, or type of literature, it belongs to.

For example, if you are writing about a Shakespearean sonnet, you may want to describe the ways it conforms to and deviates from the Elizabethan sonnet form. Does it have the proper number of lines, arranged in a typical sonnet rhyme scheme? Does its meter conform strictly to iambic pentameter? Is its imagery limited to typical sonnet conventions? Does it follow a line of argument common to sonnets? Sometimes the answer will be no. It's in the nature of texts to deviate somewhat from their generic models: often, in understanding a poem's uniqueness, we can understand the poem itself more clearly. If an author is writing within a certain genre and chooses to violate some of the "rules" of that genre, you can infer some significance from that choice.

Depending on how long the essay is to be, you may have to select a particular feature of the text to describe. Say you are writing about the formal features of *Huckleberry Finn.* You might want to describe the way Mark Twain uses dialect to characterize the people in the novel. Or you might be interested in describing the effect that Huck's narration has on the perspective of the story. Or you might look at the placement of the chapter breaks and their impact on the novel's pace. Or you might want to examine the effect of Twain's juxtaposing scenes of humor with scenes of pathos. These are only a few of the possible topics you might develop for a descriptive critical essay on this novel—pursuing any one of them will bring you closer to an understanding of how *Huckleberry Finn* works and, by extension, how novels work in general. Sometimes you can gain added insight by combining two descriptive approaches to one text: for instance, you could consider the role dialect plays in humorous scenes.

The advantage of the descriptive essay is that it gives you an entry into the workings of the text you are studying. The conventions and anticonventions you describe are not difficult to uncover and are relatively easy to defend or "prove"—there they are, in black and white, between the covers of the book. As you understand their workings in one text, you come to understand the genre more clearly. The disadvantage of writing a descriptive essay is that it can be tricky to develop your topic into an argument or thesis, an answer to the question, "So what?" When you are accounting for the obvious, as many critics so fruitfully do, some creative thinking is necessary for placing your observations in an interesting, provocative context.

The Evaluative Critical Essay

This kind of essay asks about a literary text, "Is it any good?" It's a question that has no trouble addressing the "So what?" of criticism—if the poem, play or novel is "good," it's worth reading; if it's "bad," it's a waste of time, right? What keeps evaluative criticism alive, of course, is that no two readers' standards are ever exactly the same.

The most common form of evaluative essay is the book review, of the kind professional critics write to help prospective readers decide whether to buy a book now, wait until it's out in paperback, look for it in a casual way at the library, or forget about it altogether. Teachers seldom expect students to write evaluative criticism of this kind: if a book is listed on a syllabus, the instructor undoubtedly feels it's worth reading. Sometimes, though, you may be writing to disagree with an instructor's choice; or you may want to propose a defense for a text that is not on the list. Sometimes too, instructors ask you to explain in an essay why you like or dislike a particular work they have assigned.

The number-one requirement for evaluative criticism is that you must make your standards of judgment explicit. Maybe you have a gut reaction to a particular book: reading *Pride and Prejudice* might make you feel elated or irritated, excited or bored. (I feel thrilled every time I pick it up; I know many people who retch at the thought of reading it again.) To explain why you "love" it or "hate" it, however, you need to explore the textual reasons for your response: you need to identify the formal features of texts that you do like, and compare the work in question to your model of "good literature." (What pleases me about Jane Austen, to continue the example, is the way she restricts the point of view in many scenes to her heroine's perspective—thus heightening suspense—while at the same time offering numerous hints revealing the heroine's misperceptions; I love the witty dialogue and the direct access it gives us to the characters' motives; I am continually gratified by the conventional "happy ending" she never fails to deliver.) Simply to say that you like certain features of the text is not to make an argument, however; you need to demonstrate how the text achieves the effects you admire.

Therefore, spell out your standards. If you object to the poetic form of Whitman's *Leaves of Grass,* what is the model of good poetry you contrast with it? For example: Does good poetry need rhyme and meter? Should it avoid coarse language and direct address to the reader? Why? If you admire the complexity of the narrative structure in Faulkner's "The Bear," what kind of story do you think it improves upon? For example: Are there advantages to Faulkner's scrambling chronology, quoting dialogue without clearly attributing it to characters, and otherwise departing from the conventions of more traditional short stories? Why? If you think Fitzgerald's use of symbolism in *The Great Gatsby* is effective, what ideals of symbolism are you assuming? For example: Should symbolism be clear and repetitive, or subtle? Should symbolic images carry easily recognizable, "universal" significances, or should they be idiosyncratic and obscure? Why?

Many reviewers leave their esthetic standards implicit, operating on the assumption that all educated readers can agree upon some unspoken, universal standard of literary quality. Literary criticism, though, has become more self-conscious, recognizing that all critics' judgments are colored by their subjectivity and by the position from which they are speaking: the esthetic standards of a Chicana poet are likely to differ from those of an Oxford don, but they are no less valid. If you want to judge the artistic value of a text, then, you must be clear about your own position.

Of course, your evaluation of a literary work might depend on extraliterary elements, such as political or religious attitudes. If Kate Chopin's *The Awakening* takes a stance on women's familial duties that offends you, you need to explain your own position before you can evaluate Chopin's; the same is true if your own brand of feminism approves the attitudes you think Chopin's novel endorses. Before you can argue that a text is good or bad, you must establish the values you are following. Readers who don't share your values will be inclined to disagree with your point. The challenge of evaluative criticism is to write it persuasively, alluding to the possibilities for opposition to your argument, and answering potential objections with specific commentary on passages from the text.

The Interpretive Critical Essay

In this, the most common kind of student essay, the main question you are asking is, "What does this text mean?" As my illustrations of descriptive and evaluative arguments show, a critical essay always raises questions about meaning. To write a descriptive essay is to address the question: *How* does this work transmit meaning? To write an evaluative essay is to ask: *Why* is it worthwhile to think about this text's meaning? And to write an interpretive essay is directly to ask: *What* does this work mean? Whether the work you are interpreting is on the scale of a haiku verse or *Moby Dick,* the question is never a simple one. How you find and present a meaning will depend on the strategy of interpretation you choose to apply.

The literary-academic world is made up of what Stanley Fish has called "interpretive communities" (11). These are unofficial groups of readers who agree on the best way or ways to get at the meaning of texts. Your instructor—whether or not he or she advertises or even realizes it—belongs to one or more of these communities; so do you. The study of literature is partly the process of discovering which of the communities you want to embrace.

The chapter in this book on "Literary Criticism and Theory" will guide you in more detail through the specifics of the various current strategies (see box for brief definitions). For the purpose of writing an interpretive essay, though, it's a good idea to try to determine which strategies are operating in the class you are taking. Does the professor rely exclusively on a Marxist or a Freudian model of interpretation? Does she or he introduce elements of these schools of thought in combination with other strategies? Does he or she treat texts as products of their historical context, or approach them as timeless structures? When the instructor does "close readings" of texts, does she or he look (as formalists do) for unity and

INTERPRETIVE STRATEGIES

Formalism finds meaning in the direct relation between a text's ideas and its form, the connection between *what* a text says and the *way* it's said. Formalists may find tension, irony, or paradox in this relation, but they usually resolve it into unity and coherence of meaning.

Deconstruction, too, looks at the relation of a text's ideas to the way the ideas are expressed. Unlike formalists, though, deconstructionists find meaning in the ways the text breaks down: for instance, in the ways the rhetoric contradicts the ostensible message.

Semiotics looks at the "codes," or ways of making a text intelligible, that come into play when readers encounter texts. Semioticians attend to linguistic "signs" (connotations and denotations of words), as well as those that are outside language (typography and cover illustration of books) and those that refer to the operations of language (literary conventions).

Historical criticism finds meaning by looking at a text within the framework of the prevailing ideas and assumptions of its historical era, or by considering its contents within the context of "what really happened" during the period that produced the text.

Literary-Historical criticism finds significance in the ways a particular work resembles or differs from other works of its period and/or genre. (This interpretive strategy relies heavily on the techniques of descriptive poetics, differing from poetics in its main goal: to determine what a text means, rather than "how it means.")

Biographical criticism looks for a text's significance in terms of its author, either by comparing events and attitudes in the text with those in the author's life, or by comparing textual features with author's other works.

Political criticism looks at the ideas in a text through an explicit overlay of political ideology (for example, Marxism or some forms of feminist theory) to find meaning.

Psychoanalytic criticism adopts the systems of explanation suggested by Freud (or later theorists who have built upon Freud's work, such as Lacan or the feminist psychoanalysts) to interpret what a text signifies.

Archetypal criticism traces cultural and psychological "myths" that shape the meaning of texts.

Phenomenological Reader Response criticism analyzes the ways individual readers experience texts, to find meaning in the act of reading itself.

For fuller explanations, see Chapter 5.

coherence of meaning, or point out (as deconstructionists do) ways in which parts of the text irreconcilably contradict one another? You need not use the same interpretive strategies your professor is using. Remember, though, that you should try to be explicit about *how* you reach your conclusions on the text's meaning, especially if your strategy is different from that of your intended reader.

The best interpretive essays do three things: (1) They establish the strategy by which you, the essayist, choose to find meaning. They might do this explicitly, by saying something like "I propose to do a Marxist reading of *Pride and Prejudice* in order to examine the assumptions about class relations exhibited in the text," or they may be more subtle, announcing the strategy through certain key words. If, for example, an essay's thesis paragraph refers to "desire," "the mirror stage," and "libidinal impulses," it is almost certainly drawing on psychoanalytic modes of interpretation. (2) They "read," or interpret, the work in question according to that strategy, giving lots of specific examples from the text. And (3) They make a point or an argument. Simply paraphrasing the work in your own words is not the same as interpreting it, because a paraphrase will not answer the question, "So what?" You need to place the work's ideas in some context, in order to write persuasively about it. Being self-consciously explicit about your interpretive strategy can help you develop a thesis.

□

Getting Started

Doubtless you will begin working on a critical essay unofficially for some time before you actually write anything. Some people do their best thinking in the shower, or on the jogging trail, or in conversation with friends. Working out a thesis in circumstances like these is not procrastination, but rather an important stage in the process of getting ready to write. To ensure that an argument will come to you early enough to be useful, however, you should pace yourself by going through certain steps on your way toward writing the paper. These steps may intersect and may be repeated at different stages of the process, but I have listed them here in the order in which I try to go through them myself, when writing literary criticism.

Take Notes.   As you read and reread the text, you should underline, highlight, star, or otherwise mark all the passages that interest you. When I am working on a long text, I keep track of the interesting passages by making notes to record page numbers for examples of themes or techniques that appeal to me. I like to make these notes on the blank pages and inside covers of my paperback edition of the text. This way I don't lose them, and I'm always glad to recover my previous work when I return to the same text for another project. (See this book's Chapter 2 for more advice on collecting data by "indexing" a text.)

Use Your Journal.   If you are keeping a reading journal, either by choice or assignment, it will be an ideal source of inspiration (see Chapter 1).

Ask Questions.   As you read, consult your own intellectual and emotional response to the text. Watch yourself reading, and mark any parts of the text that you found especially moving, persuasive, confusing, or difficult. Write out your questions as they occur to you; for instance, "Why does this passage make me cry?" or "Why is this description so difficult to visualize?" or "What is this novel's position on racism?" or "Why is this dialogue so hilarious?" Such questions can lead you to a thesis for any of the three modes of critical essays I have described.

Look at the Text's Form.   Try to analyze the structure of the text. If it is a poem, consider its rhyme scheme, meter, verse form, and arrangement of ideas; if it is a novel, describe for yourself its point of view, sequence of events, chapter divisions, and narrative voice. Ask yourself: To what subgenre does the structure conform? (A text that fits the genre novel, for instance, might be a a Gothic romance, a "social problem novel," a *roman à clef,* a work of fantasy or science fiction, an epistolary novel, an "experimental novel," a work of psychological realism, a historical novel, a "novel of sentiment," a mystery novel—or, most likely, a unique combination of some features of several subgenres.) In what ways does it diverge from the expected model? (Texts always do.) What is the significance of the author's having chosen this particular structure to convey the ideas in this work? For some guidance on appropriate questions to ask about particular kinds of texts, see the chapters in this book on drama, poetry, and fiction.

Look for Familiar Moves.   Identify the literary conventions in the text. Does the sonnet's persona claim that the poem will make his beloved immortal? Does the novel's narrator say the heroine is too beautiful to describe? Does the hero of the play sometimes address himself to the audience, in asides? If so, the writers are following conventions of the genres in which they are writing. The more literature you have read, the more readily you will recognize the habits that typify the period and genre you are studying. (Chapters 2, 3, and 4 of this book will help you identify some typical conventions.) Ask yourself (and your instructor) where you have seen certain patterns of conventions before. If the work you are studying is either remarkably conventional or noticeably unconventional in any respect, this might lead you to a thesis.

Interpret Figures of Speech.   Think about any imagery or figurative language you have noticed in the text. What symbolic patterns emerge? What are the vehicle and tenor of any metaphors you find? (If you are unfamiliar with the intricacies of figurative language, consult a literary handbook or your instructor.) Is there any way to read the text as an allegory for ideas that it doesn't mention directly? Make notes of your answers: abstract ideas like these can be easy to lose track of or forget.

Look Up Unfamiliar Words.   Especially if you are working on a poem, and especially if it was written before the twentieth century, you should make sure that you understand the sense in which each word is being used. Words that appear in seventeenth-century poetry, for instance, may look like modern words, but may have carried meanings or connotations that have become obsolete. For example, when John Donne mentions "trepidation of the spheres," he does not mean that the planets are alarmed or frightened; for Donne, "trepidation" also referred to a Ptolemaic explanation for planetary movements. The modern denotation might also be there, and might be relevant to your interpretation, but it's important not to overlook the original meaning.

The *Oxford English Dictionary,* available in every library, is the best source for the history of individual words in the language. It arranges definitions chronologically and provides many examples from literary and common language, so you can use it to determine exactly what meanings the word had during the era in which your author was writing. Even schools of criticism that question the advisability of trying to ascertain "authorial intention" concede that a precise grasp of the author's diction is essential to understanding literary works.

□

Make Connections

As you take notes and look over the passages that you have marked, try to establish any meaningful patterns among the material you have collected. How you determine the significance of these patterns (or the point that you want to make about them) will depend, of course, on the interpretive strategy or critical stance you adopt. Not coincidentally, your strategy will have shaped your selection of examples as well, so the move between the "collecting" and "connecting" steps will not be as tricky as you might think.

At the connecting stage, a good idea is to play a little game of "Jeopardy" with yourself: look at the data you've collected from the text and figure out what questions they might be the answers to. This is also the stage at which you will begin eliminating some of the data as less relevant to the questions you find yourself raising. Put those data aside, and think about them again when you must write a research paper or essay exam for this course. Concentrate for now on the patterns that emerge as you begin to think about your data in terms of your general questions.

What do I mean by looking for "patterns"? I mean that you should look at the examples you have collected and try to see what they might have in common with one another: the parallels among them will be your key to a thesis. A pattern might look perfectly consistent, or it might have irregularities. In either case, it can direct you to an argument. At this point you should try to decide whether you are most inclined to describe, evaluate, or interpret the work in your essay.

Your decision will depend on the patterns you have noticed and on your own critical inclinations. Say, for example, you are studying a sonnet and you have noticed that the meter in some lines varies drastically from iambic pentameter. If you want to interpret the sonnet and you are inclined to do a formalist reading, you can ask yourself, "Why is the metric variation appropriate to the ideas expressed in these lines? Why might the poet have wanted to draw special attention to these particular moments in the poem? How does that attention color the poem's meaning?" Or, for another example, in reading *Paradise Lost* you might have been interested in the seemingly heroic attractiveness of Satan. If you want to "deconstruct" the poem, you might begin by pursuing questions like this: Why does Milton's poem claim his purpose is 'to justify the ways of God to man,' then proceed to inspire so much admiration for the arch-enemy of man and God?

For still another example, you might want to do a feminist reading of Charles Dickens' *Great Expectations,* which could prompt you to ask questions such as this: What do the portrayals of Miss Havisham and Estella imply about relations between the sexes in mid-nineteenth-century England? (This would lead to historical criticism.) What do they reveal about Dickens' own attitudes toward women, or the attitude of the culture in which Dickens was writing? (This would inspire biographical, psychoanalytic, and/or political criticism.) Is my sympathy for them likely to be different, depending on whether I read as a woman or as a man? (This would fall under the rubric of reader response.) Try thinking about your data in terms of the questions that interest you most, and experiment with some possible answers.

"So What?": Create a Thesis

Once you have begun collecting some of your examples under the banner of one main question, you should begin to see the general answer that will account for the examples you want to use. This answer will become your thesis: the statement about the text that you will support with examples throughout your essay. The thesis statement you develop at this stage will probably not be identical to the one that controls the final draft of your paper. It will evolve as you think in more detail about your data and your question; you will be continually reconceiving and rephrasing your thesis as you draft your essay, and you will probably have to rewrite the thesis statement several times toward the end of the writing process, to make sure it reflects the argument you are making in your essay's final draft. Nevertheless, it's important to formulate your main argument now, as a tentative guide to writing your essay.

Generate Some Ideas.   This is the point where techniques of brainstorming can be very helpful, especially the approach that composition theorists have called "focused free writing." In spite of its liberated-sounding name, free writing is a strictly rule-governed exercise that can help you work through frustrating blocks which may be delaying your arrival at a thesis.

Here's the technique: write one of the questions you asked during the "collect" stage at the top of a clean piece of paper. (For example, "Why does Satan in *Paradise Lost* so often seem like the hero?") Set a timer or alarm clock to ring in five or ten minutes. Once the time period has begun, set your pen or pencil to the page and explore possible answers to that question. Write rapidly, without stopping or even slowing down, until all the time has elapsed. *Do not pause* to make corrections, cross out words, reread what you've written, or collect your thoughts. Just keep writing, and try to make as accurate a record as possible of what passes through your mind. If you can't think of anything to say, write "I can't think of anything to say," over and over, until you think of something. (This quickly becomes very boring and motivates you efficiently to *think* of something to say.)

Free writing in many ways resembles the techniques Toby Fulwiler describes in this book's chapter on journal writing, and it carries many of the same benefits. If you repeat the exercise several times, preferably over a period of a few days, you will amost certainly come up with original and arguable answers to your questions, one of which can become your thesis. The technique is tiring and leads to temporary bouts with writers' cramp. But, like aerobic exercise, it can produce benefits (such as self-discipline and a way to conquer writer's block) that are probably worth the pain.

Formulate the Thesis.   Perhaps the best way to go about developing your thesis at this point is to talk it over with others. By all means, take advantage of any in-class workshops or discussions your instructor may have planned for this purpose, but if you can, you should find as many opportunities as possible to explore your ideas for the paper in conversations. Visit your professor during office hours, make appointments with any teaching assistants or writing tutors available to you, or discuss your ideas with friends and classmates. Read your free writings to any willing listener, and talk over the possibilities for basing an argument on them.

At this juncture, one of the most useful questions you can ask of others is: What are some plausible arguments *against* the point I am trying to make? If there are no such arguments, then your point is probably too obvious and will make a weak thesis. If plausible arguments do exist, be glad. Your thesis is controversial enough to be interesting and you will want to refute or concede those arguments in the course of writing an essay that is persuasive, as all good essays should be.

Finding a thesis that is controversial will help you develop an answer to the big "So what." For instance, this statement would not make an arguable thesis: "In *The Great Gatsby,* Fitzgerald explores and examines the American Dream through the perspective of his narrator, Nick Carraway and the experience of his hero, Jay Gatsby." Anyone who has read the novel would probably agree that this statement is true—the novel does other things, too, but among the things it does are "exploring and examining the American Dream." To answer "So what?" an argumentative thesis must go into the *how* or *why,* must make a point.

Possible arguments for descriptive essays on this topic might be: "Through the use of narrative flashbacks, Fitzgerald reveals Nick's and Jay's parallel disillusionment with the American Dream," or "The symbolic images Fitzgerald associates with the American Dream combine with the movement of the plot to reveal ambivalence about the attractiveness of the Dream." Possibilities for an evaluative essay might include: "The narrator's eye for descriptive detail and ear for believable conversation make *Gatsby* an enjoyable spoof of the humorous side of the American Dream," or "Fitzgerald's tendency to slip into caricature—in the names, personalities, and appearances of his characters—prevents an otherwise realistic novel from being a serious critique of the American Dream." The possibilities for interpretive theses are endless: whatever strategy you choose, you will find yourself accounting for *how* or *why* Fitzgerald does what he does with the American Dream in this novel. For instance, a biographical critic might argue, "Jay Gatsby's pursuit of the American Dream parallels Fitzgerald's own experience and predicts his personal fate"; a historical critic might say, "The treatment of the American Dream in *Gatsby* simultaneously exemplifies and exposes prevailing attitudes in the 1920s toward the equation of prosperity with happiness." A feminist critic given to archetypal criticism might argue that "The portrayals of Daisy Fay and Jordan Baker as bitch-goddesses points to the misogyny at the heart of Fitzgerald's American Dream." For each of these theses there are potential counterarguments.

106

None of them is safely "right" or strictly "wrong"—their strength will depend on the quality of evidence you bring to bear in proving them.

When you think you know what you want to argue, write the thesis out in as coherent a form as possible. You may not want to state it so directly in your essay, but you should have a firm idea of it in your own mind and in your notes. This is as true for someone writing a scholarly book as for someone writing a critical essay: you need a clear, interesting answer to the question "What's it about and why does it matter?"

When you eventually do develop the thesis into an introduction for your essay, remember to phrase it in an arguable form. If you shrink from beginning an essay with a statement such as "In this essay I will argue that Fitzgerald uses the color green in *The Great Gatsby* to symbolize hope, envy, and the future," your instincts are good. Such a sentence is not a thesis: it is an announcement of the paper's topic. Instead, try to make a direct statement about how or why Fitzgerald uses the symbol, along the lines of the examples I proposed above. This would be a debatable statement, and therefore a thesis or an argument. But it doesn't need a label like, "My thesis is x" or "In this essay I will argue y." In a short critical paper, self-reference isn't necessary and can sometimes be too obvious.

This is not to say, however, that you shouldn't use the word "I." Not every professor would agree with me, but I think you should use it. Why pretend to be objective? Since your argument depends in every way on your selections—of a topic, of examples, of interpretive strategies—it has to reflect you, and it should be written in a voice that is recognizably yours. If you are making a statement that refers to your own experience, your own feeling, your own judgment, it only makes sense to attribute it to yourself. Remember, however, that (unless you are writing a particularly subjective kind of reader response criticism) *you* are not the topic of the paper, even if you are its "subject"; the poem, play, story, or novel is the object you have in view, and your essay should focus attention on the text, rather than on itself. And even if you can't be objective as you write about a text, you can and should be logical. Try, therefore, not to fall back on using "I" as an excuse for faulty reasoning: rather than using disclaimers such as "I'm not really sure, but I get the feeling that Fitzgerald is trying to say something about the American Dream . . .," work on figuring out what you do think about the topic and presenting appropriate evidence to support your idea.

Organize the Essay

Unless you've had so much experience writing from formal outlines that you are addicted to using them, don't make yourself do it. Instead, arrange your ideas informally, in a list or even a chart or map, to sketch out the order in which you want to bring them up. This will allow you the flexibility to develop new connections and slants on your examples as you write.

Shape your Argument.   Decide now what rhetorical strategy you will use in the arrangement of your essay. Will it be deductive—that is, begin with a general statement of your point, then proceed to illustrate it with specific examples arranged around subpoints? Or will it be inductive, arguing through specific examples that "build" to a concluding statement?

Some student writers prefer the inductive form for the element of suspense it injects into essays, but I suspect that few teachers appreciate the approach. If you arrange your argument deductively, you make it much easier for your reader to determine how well you are making your point. You also give the impression that you know what you are talking about from the start.

For the strongest rhetorical effect in a deductive essay, you can follow certain conventions for arranging your evidence. Put the most convincing points in the most memorable positions: the beginning and the end of the argument. Less persuasive evidence can be "buried" in the middle. You have to consult your own conscience as to whether each piece of evidence is strong enough to be used at all.

Build in Transitions.   In determining the order of your arguments, you should also think about the transitions you can make among individual points. Sometimes the same example will illustrate two points; if so, it would be a good "pivot" between them. Sometimes one of your points will qualify, alter, or even contradict another. Take these relations among your ideas into account as you work out the initial organization.

Don't Suppress Conflict.   If you find that your argument doesn't "work" perfectly, that certain aspects of the text cannot be reconciled with it or that in some ways it is self-contradictory, do your best not to ignore or bury the problem. Confront it, think about it, write about it—you may even decide to incorporate it into the final draft. I believe that a paper which recognizes, acknowledges, and attempts to deal with its difficulties is much more interesting and valuable for the writer and the reader than a paper which oversimplifies issues in order to gloss over problems. Writing literary criticism is never easy. It's perfectly all right for an essay to reflect this fact of academic life, as long as it does so intelligently and self-consciously.

□

Conventions of Writing on Literary Topics

Of course, once you have settled on an argument and a basic organization for your paper, you will write the critical essay as you would any formal written assignment: everything you know about composing, revising, and editing holds true for writing about literature. There are only a few respects in which the actual writing of literary criticism may diverge from your writing in other fields.

Verb Tense

When writing about actions that occur in a literary work, use the present tense ("Hamlet cannot decide whether to take action," not "Hamlet could not decide . . ."). When writing about events that occurred in history, use the past tense ("Shakespeare composed his plays for a dramatic company in which he sometimes acted."). When attributing ideas to an author through what he or she says in a literary work, use the present tense ("Shakespeare writes that 'all the world's a stage'.").

Quotations

Be sure that quotations are perfectly accurate: check them against the text. If a quotation is four or more lines long, indent each line ten spaces from the left margin in order to set the passage off from your own prose. When you indent a quotation, omit the quotation marks. If it is shorter than four lines, enclose it in quotation marks and treat it typographically as part of your own sentence. If you quote fewer than four consecutive lines from a poem, indicate the line breaks with a slash (/).

In writing about literature, as in all kinds of writing, you should be very careful, when you use quotations, to integrate them into your argument. Introduce every quotation from a primary source with at least one sentence or phrase that establishes its connection to what you have said in the paragraph so far (use phrases such as "in a typical example," or "in one exceptional case," or "for instance"). Then, after reproducing the quotation, be sure to comment on it specifically, pointing out the details that support your argument (this might mean paraphrasing the quotation in your own words to relate it to your argument, or it might mean drawing your reader's attention to the text's use of certain vocabulary, images, rhetorical moves, metric variations, or whatever you mean to highlight by using the quotation).

Documentation and Use of Sources

Consult the new *MLA Handbook for Writers of Research Papers* (third edition) for the simplest, most streamlined rules of documentation in literary essays. Generally speaking, a critical essay should have few or no footnotes. List the editions you are using under "Works Cited" at the end of the paper. Directly after each quotation you use as evidence, give the page number (for fiction), line number (for poetry), or act, scene and line number (for drama) in parentheses. Punctuate your sentences containing quotations like this:

> We can tell that Gulliver has passed beyond the boundaries of reason when he rejects the kindly advances of the humane Portuguese captain: "I only desired he would lend me two clean shirts, which having been washed since he wore them, I believed would not so much defile me" (337).

Remember to comment on the quotation after citing it; be sure to specify your reasons for claiming the quotation makes the point you claim it makes.

If you paraphrase ideas you found in other critics' work without quoting them directly, be careful to avoid charges of plagiarism by attributing the ideas to their source within your essay. You can use a formula like: "As Mary Poovey has pointed out, early nineteenth-century women's novels tend simultaneously to reinforce and to subvert the image of the 'Proper Lady.' " (You should attribute ideas and phrases to critics who have published work on them, even if the idea occurred to you before reading the criticism. See the chapters by James Holstun and Richard Sweterlitsch for more detailed advice on avoiding indirect plagiarism.) If you are paraphrasing a general idea from someone else's work, you will list the secondary source under "works cited" at the end of your essay. If you are borrowing a phrase or idea that occurs on a particular page, you will give that page number in parentheses in your text—"(Poovey 38)." If your context makes it clear which writer's work you are referring to, you can eliminate the author's name and give just the page number: "(38)."

Following the new MLA format, you use superscript footnotes or endnotes *only* for "content notes" that explain, qualify, or elaborate upon points in your essay that you do not want to develop within the body of the paper. Remember, the traditional footnote form that relied on *ibid.* and *op cit.,* so difficult to compose and so tiresome to follow, is obsolete in literary studies. Learn to operate within the new system. Once you've mastered it, documentation becomes much easier for both the writer and the reader to use (see Chapter 10, Writing Research, for more information on documentation).

□

Why Are You Writing a Critical Essay?

Admittedly, the process I am describing requires an enormous amount of time, energy, and concentration. Perhaps you doubt that all these steps are really what instructors expect from you when they tell you to "write a paper." I am willing to concede that we don't always *expect* to find evidence of all this work when we sit down to grade a paper, but I think most of us do *hope* to find it. From our point of view it's the process of writing a paper that will contribute to your education, more than the product that comes out of that process. A polished student essay is valuable primarily as a sign of the work and thought that went into it.

Why, after all, do you write critical essays? The superficial answer is "to fill a requirement; to earn a grade." But why do we grade you on this particular assignment? Why are critical essays such an important part of the English curriculum, taking priority in most courses over quizzes and exams? A high grade on an examination signifies mastery of the material of a course, but a high grade on an essay shows that you have mastered the modes of thought that operate in literary studies as a discipline. Your knowledge of narrative forms and poetic devices, of authors' lives and literary periods, will probably have no direct relevance to what you do in later life, unless you teach English (as only a small minority of students of literature decide to do). But your mastery of literary thinking, of the ways that critics approach and decipher texts, is an important indicator of the flexibility of your mind. And writing critical essays is the best way—in some courses, the only way—both to develop and express that mastery.

□

Works Cited

Culler, Jonathan. *The Pursuit of Signs: Semiotics, Literature, Deconstruction.* Ithaca: Cornell UP, 1981.

Fish, Stanley. *Is There a Text in This Class?* Cambridge: Harvard UP, 1980.

Gibaldi, Joseph, and Walter S. Achtert. *MLA Handbook for Writers of Research Papers,* 3rd ed. New York: The Modern Language Association, 1988.

CHAPTER 7

Writing Personal Essays

Mary Jane Dickerson

□

It was only after I descended from the trees, and tasted the joys and sorrows of becoming a scientist, that I began to meditate upon the magic city and to see in it a mirror image of the big world that I was entering. I was plunged into the big world abruptly, like Philip. The big world, wherever I looked, was full of human tragedy. I came upon the scene and found myself playing roles that were half serious and half preposterous. And that is the way it has continued ever since.

Beginning with the vivid memory of this early childhood reading of Edith Nesbit's novel *The Magic City*, Freeman Dyson narrates his development as a nuclear scientist in terms of the many interrelationships that exist between his life and his reading. In *Disturbing the Universe*, Dyson writes his autobiography as a scientist against the act of reading Nesbit's book and many others as he was growing up in England. Writing personal essays in response to literature often assumes such autobiographical frames of reference.

This kind of personal essay resembles the human voice talking just as the mind works—in a natural outpouring without the more systematic ordering of ideas usually associated with literary criticism. Indeed, each act of writing may generate a difference in perspective and voice according to the needs and the constraints of the particular piece of writing because each of us possesses many selves. Behind every essay about literature there exists such an "I" informing the whole.

Learning how to place yourself at the center of writing about literature gives you ways to speak to audiences beyond students and professors. Since this essay writing is exploratory in nature rather than expository, you are able to discover your personal connections with the literature you study in order to make these works and their words a part of your life. This process of discovery is what you make real through putting it into words— or, to put it another way, in the personal essay you combine what you think with what you are. Such a personal approach to writing about literature has a long history in the literary essay that continues today as people delight in sharing the pleasures of reading poetry, fiction, nonfiction, and drama. From the sharp wit of Addison and Steele in the eighteenth century decrying such poetic practices as composing poems in the shapes of wings and altars to the genial and open tones of John Updike as he describes our times through what he reads and shares with us, personal responses to reading enlarge the possibilities of literature.

□

Creating a New Text

Since the personal response to a text merges the act of reading with the activity of making an essay, you also have the opportunity to create literature through the discovery of the "I" in your prose—who you are in relationship to what you are writing about. It happened to one student of mine as she reflected on being an English major against the texts and contexts she has met along the way. Here is the opening paragraph of Maureen's essay "Women's Studies: My Right to an Education":

> It seems my education has always been strictly divided into male and female subjects. I remember in high school telling my mother that I might be interested in being a veterinarian. She frowned at this and told me that I wouldn't really like being around sick animals. I began to wonder if my fondness for biology was abnormal because even though dissecting a crayfish was not a milestone in my life, my parents trivialized my enthusiasm about it in comparison to the praise they lavished on my maudlin poetry and oil paintings. While my parents and teachers forgave my incompetence in mathematics, they encouraged my interest in literature.

Maureen's life experience—her story—sets up an autobiographphical frame of reference for the story of her educational experience.

In the following paragraph, Maureen's personal experience merges with what she has read to create a richer context for synthesizing meanings and implications for women studying a body of literature largely determined by and taught by men.

My college introductory course in British and American literature contained a token selection of poems and essays by women. While we spent four classes on Wordsworth's *Prelude,* we only spent one class on Virginia Woolf. While we read Hemingway's *The Sun Also Rises,* we ignored *Jacob's Room, The Waves,* and *To the Lighthouse.* Instead, we read Woolf's essays, "A Room of One's Own" and "Professions of Women." In doing so, we acknowledged Woolf as a woman who wrote and not as the innovative writer of fiction that she is. Ironically, even though Woolf has a small chapter in the *Norton Anthology of English Literature,* she can be, like Shakespeare's sister, a "lost novelist" because of the perfunctory treatment she receives in the classroom.

This essay reflects a process of intellectual integration as Maureen examines her educational experience since childhood through a lens that allows her to organize meaning in a powerful way.

Maureen has listened to the voices of the writers included in her English courses as she has listened to the voices of her family and teachers. And from the integration of these voices into her own experience, she has forged a personal perspective by writing an extended essay in which she examines how far our society has to go before all its citizens have the same rights and freedoms of education. The final paragraph of "Women's Studies: My Right to an Education" illustrates how far she's moved from the details of her own educational experience toward the kind of insight she needs to pose imaginative and important questions:

Intellectual integration from grammar school through college is most important. It took until 1948 for women to gain the legal right to learn as stated in the United Nations Declaration of Human Rights. Not only should everyone have the right to education, but "Education shall be directed to the full development of the human personality and the strengthening of respect for human rights and fundamental freedoms." I wonder how long it will take until the world decides that Women's Studies, as a discipline, should be instrumental in the development of these rights and freedoms.

In this essay, Maureen has engaged an audience beyond the confines of classroom, academic major, and even college or university.

□

My Story

As a college freshman in 1955, when I was assigned to read Faulkner's story "A Rose for Emily," I immediately recognized that not only was I reading about a character in a small town in rural Mississippi but I was also reading about a woman who lived as close as two houses down the road in my own rural North Carolina. What I was in the act of reading merged with details of my own existence. It was as if from that moment on, writing about a work of literature was no longer an abstract exercise, but held possibilities of knowing unlike any other I had ever encountered. In "A Sketch of the Past," Virginia Woolf describes this sort of experience for herself as a writer: "It is the rapture I get when in writing I seem to be discovering what belongs to what. . . . It proves that one's life is not confined to one's body and what one says and does; one is living all the time in relation to certain background rods or conceptions" (27). Since I first glimpsed these connections through reading, I have also written about those characters who peopled my childhood by filling the spaces of my poems with them. Writing and living have continued to overlap through both reading and writing.

All serious readers undergo such shocks of recognition and find themselves forever altered by what they read. No matter whether we are writing about a fictional life, an actual life, or indeed our own lives, what autobiographer Wallace Fowlie says rings true: "Writing is indeed a process of self-alteration. Living belongs to the past. Writing is the present" (275). We make connections with the voices in fiction, in autobiography, in poetry, in our own various texts, and of those people surrounding us as part of our everyday lives. We keep reading, we keep listening, and we keep writing.

William Faulkner's representations and visions of reality have offered me ways to make sense of my own "postage stamp of the universe." Perhaps you can name the writer who has done the same for you. Although I have never recovered from that powerful initiation, the "I" who writes occasionally about Faulkner and other American authors has undergone transformations and has learned to listen to the many potential and possible voices that enable writing literary criticism as well as poems, essays, letters, and journals as the need and desire arise.

□

Personal Essays

Let's pause for a moment to list some things to keep in mind when writing personal responses to literature:

- □ Autobiographical: Use "I" frequently even when autobiography is not central.

- □ Conversational: Create a friendly sense of equality between yourself and your reader (or audience).

- Exploratory: Be reflective, even imaginative, rather than explanatory or analytical (or persuasive).

- Creative: Whenever appropriate, consider how reflecting on the act of writing might allow you to participate in the creative process of the literary work—in the production of meaning itself.

- Open: Rather than coming to a conventional kind of conclusion that ties things together, try, instead, to follow where the central idea might lead you toward other possibilities, thereby encouraging the play of ideas that resists the finality of usual conclusion or closure.

Of course, not all personal essays about literature exhibit each of these features, but I think you'll find many of them present in contemporary essays published in places like *The New York Review of Books, The New York Times Book Review, The Georgia Review,* and *The New Yorker,* to name only a few major publications. Here's a recent example from *The Times Book Review,* "Staying Alive by Learning to Write," an essay in which Swiss writer Adolf Muschg reflects on the exclusion of the writer and "creative writing" from the Swiss university:

> Until fairly recently, for a European professor to admit that he or she was secretly doing some "creative writing" was tantamount to academic suicide. One could do serious work *on* writing or writers, but they had better be dead. Knowing something about current literature, if you claimed to be a scholar, implied the proud modesty of not even trying your own hand at it—or it would wither from the sacrilege.
>
> I happen to write and teach German literature. . . . (1)

From the beginning, Muschg engages our attention from his own perspective as both teacher and writer in the university.

□

Autobiography

To stimulate a rich identification between students and their literary subjects, I often distribute an autobiographical questionnaire to help students generate their responses during the entire semester as part of their course journal. For my literature courses, autobiography encourages students to connect the narratives they see within their own lives to the narratives that they are reading in various literary genres. Responding to these questions can stimulate richly conceived essays in which you actively integrate your experience into your interpretation of others' texts. Questions about the self can arm you with a powerful invention tool to create textual forms that may more uniquely represent your writerly identity. At least, posing such questions is worth a try. Here is a list of questions that you can use as a guideline and add to as you read.

□

Autobiographical Questionnaire

1. Is there any dominant physical trait, gesture, or feature in a character that gives you special insight into yourself? Of others close to you? How does this recognition affect your response to the character? The work?

2. Is there a character who comes close to being like you in important ways? Describe the similarities.

3. What physical objects in your reading do you associate with yourself, your parents, or other family members? What does their appearance make you think about?

4. What things that you are most passionate about appear in your reading? How does this recognition affect your response?

5. What of your major fears do you also find in literary characters? What inhibitions or desires?

6. What patterns or events in your own life are reflected in the literature you are reading? What similarities and/or differences are there in the events selected?

7. What are the motivating forces of your own life that set up particular responses to the literary work?

8. Which place or setting (interior, landscape, street, building) in your reading do you identify with most and why?

9. What have you found most disturbing or disquieting (or pleasurable and satisfying?) about what you are reading? Why?

10. What connections do you see between some aspect of political or social life in the present and political and social life in an earlier work?

11. How do you see the past affecting the present in your own life? In the lives of characters you are reading about?

12. What is your earliest memory of reading or being read to? Do you remember the book's title? What are your favorite books

and the ones that remain most vividly a part of you? How might these earlier reading experiences have affected your responses to literature in the present?

What follows are some journal explorations students have made in response to the autobiographical questionnaire; in each case, the writer found possibilities for the personal essay. One student describes his obsession with running in answer to the question about being altered in some way by what he is reading, in this case Annie Dillard's *A Pilgrim at Tinker Creek:*

> The syllable ME was not the center of my thoughts this fine October afternoon. Orange, red, and brown captured my imagination. I stared at the sun through the trees. Looking up at the sun, patches of color registered in my head. I felt daring enough to close my eyes for an instant; imprinted on my eyelids were kaleidoscopic images of the leaves. The death grey bark of the white birch, which is my favorite tree, reminded me of winter. I had found my own "tree with the lights in it." It had come in the form of loosely connected observances and recollections. My "tree" was not as profound or cohesive as Dillard's, but that did not matter. It was my own.
>
> Adrian

This material from his own daily experience finally turned into an exploratory essay titled "Running After Dillard," in which Dillard's book altered Adrian's running attitudes and habits.

In another journal entry, a student describes the experience of hearing Hayden Carruth read his own poetry:

> I had never gone to hear a poet speak or read his poetry before in person. But I got what I expected. I expected to feel special because I was in the same room as an excellent poet. I expected to hear other works not in the book we read and to get more meaning from poems I had already read because he would be speaking the voice that originally spoke them before they were written down on paper.
>
> You know, after reading the above paragraph I wonder about myself. My ability to communicate is almost nonexistent in that paragraph.
>
> Brian

Most of us would probably disagree with Brian and regard his intense experience of seeing, hearing, and remembering coupled with the writing and reading in his journal as a revelation of what it means to experience a poetry reading. Using oneself as a vehicle to explore the meanings of literary texts makes reading a co-creative act: acts of reading *and* writing the self. Brian later wrote an essay in which he used his own knowledge and performance of jazz to explore its influence on the composition of many of Carruth's poems in *Brothers, I Loved You All.*

□

Conversation

Since writing about literature is like engaging in a personal dialogue with writers and their texts—as both Maureen and Muschg do throughout their essays—this sense of conversation, with its strong use of "I," creates a friendly relationship between writer and audience. One of the most powerful places for such dialogues to occur is in the journals described in Chapter 1. The many and varied conditions of journal writing provide an even larger framework that encourages free-ranging writing activities that involve the self. It's as if the autobiographical journals create ideal conditions for conversations to take place between you and what you're reading—between who you are and what you think. These conversations, in turn, help bridge the gap between reading and writing that all of us experience to some degree whenever we are faced with a writing assignment.

When we write as frequently as we read, we enlarge our potential to make connections with facets of our own lives. Many writers acknowledge the pleasure they get when readers communicate just how much their works have affected their lives. Surely Alice Walker would appreciate what this reader expresses in a journal entry about how sharing *The Color Purple* with her mother enriched that reading experience for her:

> I haven't had much in common with my mother for a while, and that seemed to crumble away this weekend. She has read *The Color Purple* and we spent the whole day talking about women, her relationship with my father, her job, her education and all that she feels about such things. For the first time in a while I found myself caring about her thoughts and listening to what she said. She talked about the book and how she would like to borrow mine to read more by Alice Walker. I told her that I would send her some of her own which I promptly did when I got back to Burlington. I sent her *Once* and inscribed it with one of A. W.'s musings from "Mississippi Winter II":
>
>> When you remember me, my child,
>> be sure to recall that Mama was
>>
>>   . . . . .
>>   not happy
>> with fences.

119

> I think I started to really love my mother again this
> weekend.
>
>   Patti

For Patti, discussing her reading of Alice Walker encourages her to engage in conversation with communities of voices outside those she hears in the novel: she creates an informing context to enrich her own reading experience. Through reflection on the novel in her journal, she gets in touch with her own mother's life and reestablishes a vital connection.

Alice Walker's voice sets into play the voices of a mother and daughter that found an outlet through a journal entry. But what's even more significant here is that the student's major piece of writing for the semester turned into an examination of the nurturing and inspiring influence that earlier writer Zora Neale Hurston has had on the contemporary writer Alice Walker—another variation of mother-daughter relationships. For Patti, reflecting on the role of family as she reads Walker, whose fiction and poetry speak to all women as they explore their bonds with both their real and their adopted mothers, provides her with a perspective for writing an essay about Hurston's influence on Walker. The thematic concern in the journal entry provides the central thematic concern in an essay in which Patti traces the intertextual relationships that exist between Zora Hurston's *Their Eyes Were Watching God* and Alice Walker's *The Color Purple.* Through using your journal as the site for personal explorations about the literature you read, you practice the kinds of conversations that enable you to speak about yourself in the act of reading in equally powerful ways.

☐

Exploration

Since you may not be trying to prove a point about a literary work, the form of the personal essay may take on a different shape than the exposition you are more accustomed to in which you develop a thesis and marshal support toward a persuasive and reasoned conclusion. Consider the following scenario. Your teacher might make an assignment similar to one given recently in a British literature course when the teacher asked students to write a personal response to their reading of a Wordsworth poem. This assignment demanded a careful reading of the poem, but the interpretation must also be informed by the student's own life.

In response to Wordsworth's urging that we can learn much of value from nature in "Expostulation and Reply," you might open your essay with a description of a memorable instance of productive inner reflection or daydreaming. From this personal anecdote, you might compare the progress of Wordsworth's own process of learning from nature in a state of daydreaming as he narrates it in his poem. You might interweave other scenes from your own childhood and schooling that show how children learn from their environments as well as from formal education. In the ending of your essay, you might speculate on what we might learn from Wordsworth's poem as contemporary educators consider lengthening the school day and going to a year-round schedule.

For a similar kind of assignment, another student recognizes in Maxine Hong Kingston's *Woman Warrior: Memoir of a Chinese Childhood Among Ghosts* implications for his own cultural identity:

> Since I am a third generation Chinese-American, I am further removed than Kingston from a Chinese past. Both of my parents speak Chinese, but I lost my ability to speak Chinese as I grew up . . . and now I am unable to have any lengthy conversation with my grandmother. She does not speak English and I do not speak Chinese. We communicate through limited vocabulary and creative sign language. . . . I really feel a tremendous loss. Now I am learning the Chinese language and searching for my roots. For the first time in my life I am considering myself Chinese.
>
> Jason

As Jason considered his reading of his own life alongside reading Kingston's memoir, his choice of representing himself as author through the writerly "I" became a natural, even an inevitable, act as he faced the dimension of loss in his own life. He could not write an authentic critical essay about the nature of Maxine Hong Kingston's search for gender, familial, and cultural identity without exploring and acknowledging his own Chinese-American history. It's as if these autobiographical connections create the conditions for conversations to take place between writers and readers so that readers also become writers of their own stories in the flexible form of the personal essay.

Writer Julian Barnes creates these conditions as he explores the sequence of events that led him to write a novel about Flaubert rather than another biography in his essay "The Follies of Writer Worship":

> I once owned a piece of Somerset Maugham's gate. Well, not exactly Somerset Maugham's gate—it wasn't pillaged from the Villa Mauresque—but near enough. My chunk of literary wood came from the vicarage at Whitstable where Maugham spent part of his unhappy childhood. (1)

From the spar of Maugham's gate, Barnes proceeds to the mystery of two stuffed parrots, each alleged to be the inspirations for Flaubert's short story "A Simple Heart." From the mystery of the parrots, he moves toward the process of discovery he himself undergoes as he ponders how best to use his research about Flaubert. The creative process of the essay reflects the creative process of making the fiction resulting in Barnes's own novel, *Flaubert's Parrot.* At the essay's close, Barnes reminds us of his beginnings and anticipates what might lie ahead for one who indulges in "The Follies of Writer Worship":

> I no longer own my spar of Somerset Maugham's gate. It disappeared in a move, or was burned by mistake or stolen to patch someone else's gate. Besides, I am no longer quite so keen on Maugham. But I have something else now, an odder and more poignant trophy—an unopened packet of Disque Bleu that was found at Arthur Koestler's elbow after his suicide two years ago. The cigarettes sit on a shelf a few feet from my desk. I look at them from time to time. . . . (8)

Just as Julian Barnes's essay illustrates, whenever we write, we are engaged in making meanings, but these meanings are never fixed or static on the page (or on the screen or the world, for that matter); they become texts constantly undergoing construction as readers read and remake them through the lenses of their own representations of reality. Writing through such awareness of what happens is akin to what Joan Didion describes in the opening lines of her essay, "Why I Write":

> Of course I stole the title for this talk from George Orwell. One reason I stole it was that I like the sound of the words: *Why I Write.* There you have three short unambiguous words that share a sound, and the sound they share is this:
> I
> I
> I (257)

Didion continues the exploration of her preoccupation with the sound of her own voice and its significance for her identity as a writer. By acknowledging her debt to Orwell's essay, she places herself in the company of those who see writing as a process of creating the "I".

□

Engaging the Creative Process

Student Charles Baraw took full advantage of the creative process to shape an essay he called "Purgatory," in which he writes his own autobiography against reading Virginia Woolf's *A Room of One's Own* and Dante's *Divine Comedy.* Here is how he opens the piece: "Virginia Woolf—that was the name embossed on the tattered binder of the slim black book. It was strange the significance the name and the book had taken in my life."
    Baraw traces his memory of hearing about this book from earlier high

school years when "I was excited to add her to my growing list of 'must reads.' She joined Milton, Melville, and Hemingway." In college, Hemingway remained prominent while Woolf remained unread, but Baraw's involvement with women friends whose growing interests in feminist ideas and issues began to affect him as well—often in spite of himself: "A few months later Deidre took *A Room of One's Own* out [of the library] in my name, read it, and left it on my desk. I asked her about it. I wanted her to sum up the answers it contained and hand them to me ready for consumption." After a period of time had passed with the loss of Deidre as lover and friend, Virginia Woolf's book remained as yet unread until "I started to read" these words: " 'But, you may say, we asked you to speak about women and fiction—what has that got to do with a room of one's own?' I nearly slammed the book shut in my shock. What was this woman doing—talking directly to me? I hadn't asked anything. Shouldn't she just leave me alone and let me read her story and take it as I wish? Something was obviously wrong here."

He examines his own relationships with and attitudes toward women through his responses to the constant sound of Virginia Woolf's voice. The autobiographical essay takes on the shape of a dialogue between aspiring male writer and authoritative female writer—a kind of lesson of the master as mistress, with Charles in the role of Dante, Virginia Woolf in the role of Virgil:

```
Virginia Woolf, with her casual yet firm voice, seemed
to be offering her hand to anyone who was willing to un-
dertake the journey. Convinced I would not reach the end
without her as my guide, I took hold of her hand. Mine was
sweaty.

No sooner had we begun than Virginia asserted, "Fiction
here is likely to contain more truth than fact. . . . I
need not say what I am about to describe has no exis-
tence."

I squeezed her hand tighter—no existence—for she
deemed the earth below my feet to be imaginary, and it
sank away. Before my vertigo subsided, I found we were
walking along the venerable turf of Oxford University,
surrounded by its ancient buildings, sacred churches,
and revered libraries—this was something of a comfort.
```

In this excerpt we can see how Charles Baraw makes use of the imagined experience to mingle with details of his reality and the language of Woolf's text to organize meaning into a text of his own.

Several features distinguish the textual form of "Purgatory" in addition to its literary allusions and resonances. First, the author keeps the piece firmly grounded in place. He describes his scene of reading as follows and keeps referring to that place until the end of reading *A Room of One's Own*:

I picked it up one day, and lay beneath a tall, strong
maple tree which was caressed by an unusually brilliant
sun. Its leaves were just beginning to ignite; some on
top were unusually bright red, and the rest were in various stages of combustion—orange, yellow, and green. I
was as happy as I could hope, under the circumstances,
under the tree on the thick grass on a fine September
day.

I started to read.

The second most important feature of Charles's essay is the way he
relies on dialogue to advance the narrative and its revelatory power. The
central dialogue is the one he carries on with Virginia Woolf as his mentor,
using her actual language in combination with his imagined (yet real!)
language:

All through lunch Virginia's insistent question, "why,
why are men so angry?" rang in my head. It was driving me
crazy. Meanwhile Virginia read the newspaper. Suddenly
she announced, "The most transient visitor to this
planet must see that England is under the rule of a patriarchy." I perked up. The ringing question stopped.
This was common ground. I agreed enthusiastically,
remembering my paper on Milton, *"Paradise Lost:* A Poetical Rationalization of Patriarchy." Yes, the domi-
nation of women is a key to upholding social
hierarchies, the state, and. . . .

The dialogue with Virginia Woolf and the memories of and references
to other writers are constantly punctuated by Charles's dialogues with his
sister and with Deidre and other women in his life. In these remembered
conversations, Baraw realizes the many connections between Woolf's
words and his own relationships with women and his attitudes about male
and female in art and as artists.

Virginia returned to the question. Why are men angry?
Her calm voice shattered my careful logical constructions. "Life for both sexes . . . is arduous, difficult,
a perpetual struggle . . . it calls for confidence in
oneself. And how can we generate this imponderable
quality most quickly? By thinking that people are inferior to oneself?" I nearly choked. . . . "Women have
served all these centuries as looking-glasses possess-
ing the magic and delicious power of reflecting the figure of man at twice the natural size."

Sheri, my little sister, not yet five, sat across from me
on the floor. She looked in a toy mirror and pretended to
apply makeup. I sauntered over and knocked it out of her
hands.

True to memory and true to the way memory operates in time, the third feature Baraw's writing displays so vividly is that, although a narrative, his autobiography moves around in time so that the contemporary consciousness becomes intrinsic to the development of the self. He writes:

```
Virginia kept pushing further and further, memory after
memory crowded my mind.

"The looking-glass vision is of supreme importance be-
cause it changes the vitality; it stimulates the ner-
vous system. Take it away and a man may die like a drug
fiend deprived of his cocaine."

COCAINE! cooo-caine. . . . Karla, my high school girl-
friend . . . sat on my bed. . . .

"Yeh, Karla, let's do another line—I still have to write
that paper."

"But I have to drive home, and the roads are terrible."
```

This scene also continues as Baraw recognizes yet another painful instance of his exploitation of women, especially with regard to writing—a recurring theme in this self-examination.

Moving around in time and evoking many voices in literature and in his own life in fully developed scenes and settings enable Baraw to create a textual form that, although clearly linked to what writers in the past from Dante to Woolf have done with the actual circumstances of their own lives, expresses what he sees himself as being at this time in his education. It's a marvelous blend of reader response literary criticism and of autobiography that calls the self into being while making a text. Through writing "Purgatory," with its intertextual resonances with Dante and with Woolf, Baraw expands his knowledge of autobiography as literature, the lives of women and men as writers, and the emerging contours of his own capacity for creating voices through which to give voice to his world.

□

Open-Ended

While it may not be appropriate on all writing occasions to use "I" as personally as I have shown it being used in this chapter, knowing more ways to incorporate your own life experience into the life of what you read whenever you write about literature gives you more choices about which voice to select for expressing yourself. Much of what I've suggested is close to William Stephany's advice in his chapter, "Imaginative Writing and Risk Taking." Much of what I've suggested also has links to Toby Fulwiler's "Journal Writing" and Robyn Warhol's "Writing Critical Essays."

It's as if the personal response to literature falls somewhere between the informality of journal writing and the more formal structures of the critical essay.

Perhaps I've altered the way you will regard yourself as a writer about literature while you are reading literature. You are, after all, an author whenever you write, and just *who* you are signifies a great deal for your ongoing process of self-creation. The autobiographical element in all texts is what makes each of us anxious when we show what we have written to another reader, no matter how sympathetic that reader might be: it is always as if we are being judged along with our words—our words *are* us in an important way as we seek to join a community of readers and writers through literary study. Writing autobiographically is exploratory and, for that reason, risky. You may often ask, as Charles Baraw does at the end of his essay, "But how, how, I wondered, would I squeeze this onto paper? Virginia Woolf had one more answer. 'So long as you write what you wish to write, that's all that matters, and whether it matters for ages or hours, nobody can say.' I walked on."

□

Works Cited

Barnes, Julian. "The Follies of Writer Worship." *The Best American Essays 1986.* Ed. Elizabeth Hardwick and Robert Atwan. New York: Ticknor & Fields, 1986.

Didion, Joan. "Why I Write." *Eight Modern Essayists.* Ed. William Smart. 4th ed. New York: St. Martin's 1985.

Dyson, Freeman. *Disturbing the Universe.* New York: Harper, 1979.

Fowlie, Wallace. "On Writing Autobiography." *The Southern Review* 22 (1986): 273–279.

Muschg, Adolf. "Staying Alive by Learning to Write." *New York Times Book Review* 1 Feb. 1987: 1, 27–28.

Woolf, Virginia. "A Sketch of the Past." *Eight Modern Essayists.* Ed. William Smart. 4th ed. New York: St. Martin's 1985.

CHAPTER 8

Imaginative Writing and Risk Taking

William A. Stephany

In most cases, writing an analytical or interpretive paper will be the way you can best demonstrate the quality of your reading and thinking about a work of literature. However, if that is by far the most common and usually the most appropriate form for your writing, it is by no means the only one. There may be times when the best way for you to respond to a work might be to write a parody or an imitation of it or to write some other form of imaginative or playful paper. Recently, when I assigned a paper in a survey of British literature, in addition to four traditional topics for analytical essays, I offered students the following option:

Congratulations! You have just been awarded a one-month trial membership in the Scriblerus Club. Now that you have read some of the works of your fellow club members Jonathan Swift and Alexander Pope, perhaps you would like to try your hand at a similar act of creation. Per-

haps you would like to bring Lemuel Gulliver out of re-
tirement and compose a portion of his fifth voyage, one
which would reveal something about *our* world. Or perhaps you have found some of the lost couplets of Alexander Pope, originally intended for inclusion in *any* of
his poems assigned for class.

Or perhaps you'd like to try your hand at a parody of the
conventions, style, or concerns of *any* writer or work
covered this semester. Try your hand at a metaphysical
conceit or Miltonic blank verse or heroic couplets. Remember that parodists often strive for a disparity between content and parodied form: part of the fun of the
Dunciad and "Rape of the Lock" lies in the heroic treatment of inherently non-heroic subjects.

In response to this assignment, several students wrote chapters from
an imagined fifth Book of *Gulliver's Travels,* and most of them did an excellent job of maintaining a tone akin to Swift's. One, for example, caught
the spirit of Swift's use of gratuitous detail to imply, tongue-in-cheek, that
these clearly fantastic voyages actually happened:

> . . . I left with a crew of sixty-five aboard the *Devon-
> shire* well equipped for most difficulties I would en-
> counter. It had been four years since my last voyage.
> . . . First mate Lou Noonford spotted land at 3:15 on the
> twenty-second day, so we sailed south until we reached
> the rocky shore where we were met by what appeared to be
> a friendly fisherman.

> Andy

Only someone who had entered into the pleasure of reading *Gulliver's
Travels* could emulate the style in this way. Because of the way it brings
one element of the work to the foreground, Andy's imitation may itself be
considered a form of interpretation.

An imaginative paper can also demonstrate an understanding of a
work's thematic concerns. In his version of a fifth book, another student,
Jim, extended one of the patterns through which Swift presents Gulliver's
increasing misanthropy. In Book I, Gulliver is shipwrecked; in Book II, he
is abandoned; in Book III, he is set adrift by pirates; in Book IV, he is the
victim of mutiny. The motivation for his "journeys" gets worse and worse.
In Jim's paper, Gulliver, whom we had left hating humans and loving
horses at the end of Book IV, murders a man who is whipping a horse, and
so begins his final adventure by fleeing in an open boat from a lynch mob.

A creative response to an assigned reading can also use the form of the
original to comment on some aspect of our contemporary world. A third
student wrote about Gulliver's journey to a fictional "land of excessive
knowledge," where he encounters a native named Dalloway:

```
The inhabitants are much like humans, but supposedly
better because of their capacity to take in verbal and
written knowledge. . . . Lessons are taught by educators
who speak at sixty words per ciab. A ciab is almost equal
to ten seconds. These people have existed for nearly two
trillion years, so in each education period almost two
thousand years are covered. . . . [Knowledge] is served to
them at such a quick pace that they neither can retain,
nor recall much of it. Dalloway also conveyed to me that
the thirst for knowledge is so great that most pupils
interpret it in the wrong way.

                          Phil
```

Phil is here recalling Swift's own thematic concerns, especially in Book III, in which he satirizes inappropriate approaches to knowledge. His imagined world allows him to make his point about the frustrations of taking a lecture-format survey, one covering British literature from the seventh through the the eighteenth centuries in one semester. Since his parody is true to the spirit and form of Swift's work (and includes quotations from and mock scholarly annotations on Shakespeare), he also demonstrates how much he has learned from his reading, a technique that inherently confers credibility to his implied critique of the course format.

☐

"Rules" for Risk Taking

However attractive an option of this sort might seem, let us acknowledge from the outset that novelty of approach is no guarantee that a paper will be written well, and if you've never tried this kind of writing before, you will probably welcome some guidelines before beginning. You will realize, I assume, that none of the suggestions I'm about to make should be regarded as hard-and-fast rules for writing this kind of paper. It would be ironic for me to propose in one paragraph that you expand the possibilities for writing about literature, only to begin limiting those possibilities in the next one. I would like to describe what some of my students have done, in order to suggest the wide range of what is possible and also to generalize about why certain kinds of writing have worked.

There are, however, three principles which are so universally applicable that I'd suggest you *should* consider them to be absolute.

Careful Reading

Rule number one is important for any kind of writing about literature: *Know your subject matter.* In order to do a good job writing the kind of paper

I am proposing, you need to have read the text closely, to have thought about it deeply, to have internalized for yourself its form, its themes, its structure, its rhythms, both verbal and conceptual, its relationship to the other readings in the course. If your paper is to be effective, it must be more than just a clever reaction to the text; it must be an interpretation of it. Whether your purpose is to mimic a writer's stylistic quirks (as Andy does in his parody of *Gulliver*), or to cast light on his or her subject matter (as Jim does), or to illuminate our own world as mediated through the assigned text (as Phil does), you need a clear sense of your purpose as a writer and a solid understanding of the original text in order to write an effective paper.

Voice

Rule number two is more specifically appropriate for an imaginative paper: *Maintain a consistent voice.* If your paper requires you to adopt a voice or a point of view, don't shift ground in the middle to explain what you're doing; allow the voice to develop. Swift himself provides an excellent model for this principle in his famous essay "A Modest Proposal." As an Irish patriot, he had already written a wide range of pamphlets protesting the economic abuses England had been inflicting on Ireland in the early eighteenth century. The suggestions he made in these "analytical essays" were all ignored, so he finally circulated anonymously a pamphlet written in the style of a "Projector," the term used in his day to describe people who proposed projects for implementation of economic or social policy. In this case, the project being advanced is one which would allegedly cure the country of its crippling poverty. Only after we've read several pages of cool, deadpan calculation about the scope of the problem does the full horror of the project become clear—that the infants of the poor be fattened for the first year of their lives and then slaughtered, their meat offered for sale to the wealthy. A bit later still, the pamphlet's underlying figure of speech becomes clear: since the landlord class has been metaphorically consuming the parents, they may as well literally consume the children. The chilling effect of the whole piece depends on Swift's relentless consistency in maintaining the speaker's matter-of-fact voice. With his concentration on mathematical finesse and blind logic, the speaker implicitly condemns those like himself who would treat a human crisis as if it were an intellectual problem.

Revision

Rule number three actually applies to any kind of writing, not just to writing about literature: *Revise.* Your paper will assume its final polish and its final point only as a result of several revisions. The point seems obvious but needs to be made, since a creative paper might often begin life as a journal entry or free writing. While this might be a thoroughly appropriate and normal way for the idea, or even for an entire draft, to be generated, such a draft, if left unrevised, will almost surely be inadequate as a final paper. Be prepared for the possibility that you may be too close to your original draft immediately after completing it to assume editorial objectivity toward it: it's difficult—indeed, for most of us, it's impossible—to be creative and critical at the same time. Let at least a day pass after you've written your draft before you return to it to revise it, and then try to read it objectively, as someone else will read it. Better still, find someone else to whom you can read your work, ideally a friend who is also in the course for which you're preparing the paper. Such a person has read the text you're writing about and shares with you a familiarity with the dynamics of the class and the concepts that have been considered. As you read your paper aloud to such an audience, you will hear the parts of the paper that work well or poorly; your friend will hear more.

□

Creative Choices

There are several ways in which you might write creatively about a work of literature. Here are a few:

Imitation of Form

Parody is the term used for writing that imitates the style of another, usually famous, piece of work, and sometimes this imitation of form can be extremely close, maintaining the exact rhyme scheme of a poem, for example, or the syntax of the original's sentences.

The sixteenth-century writer Christopher Marlowe's poem, "The Passionate Shepherd to his Love," inspired two well-known parodies of this sort. Marlowe begins his poem:

> Come live with me and be my love,
> And we will all the pleasures prove
> That valleys, groves, hills, and fields,
> Woods, or steepy mountain yields. (813)

In this famous pastoral poem, Marlowe's shepherd invites his beloved nymph to live with him a simple life of uncomplicated pleasure. Several of his contemporaries wrote poems in response to Marlowe's, two of which are themselves quite famous. Walter Ralegh's "Nymph's Reply to the

131

Shepherd" repeats many of the same words and deals with many of the same concepts, but in order to make the opposite point. For Ralegh's nymph, time and deception make it impossible to accept the offer of a world without responsibilities. He begins:

> If all the world and love were young,
> And truth in every shepherd's tongue,
> These pretty pleasures might me move
> To live with thee and be thy love. (782)

If Ralegh's response is serious, John Donne's is comic. He begins his poem, "The Bait," by inviting his love to live with him so they can go fishing together:

> Come live with me and be my love,
> And we will some new pleasures prove,
> Of golden sands and crystal brooks,
> With silken lines and silver hooks. (1074)

In response to the assignment reproduced earlier in the chapter, two students wrote close parodies of poems studied during the semester, and as with Ralegh's and Donne's, one was serious, one comic. Shakespeare's Sonnet 73 appears on the next page with Melissa's parody below it.

The rhyme schemes of the two poems are the same (though the logical structure of Shakespeare's first twelve lines consist of three groups of four lines, and Melissa's consists of four groups of three). As in Shakespeare's poem, Melissa's speaker is conscious of aging and speaks of what one can see in her, but in contrast to the relatively tranquil resolution in Shakespeare's poem, where advancing age increases the intensity of love, Melissa's sonnet presents a terrifying view of aging. "In me thou seest what soon shall be thy fate," says her speaker, and the result is a rejection which isolates the elderly from loved ones.

Another student, Peter, achieves a delightfully comic effect by dealing with a relatively trivial topic in the style of a poem dealing with a serious one. John Donne's poem "The Good Morrow" celebrates the wonders of "awakening" to true sexual intimacy; Peter calls his parody, celebrating a love affair with a lawn mower, "The Good Toro"; see page 134.

Parodies

Parodies of specific works need not follow the form of the originals as closely as these examples do. Students of mine have written a wide range of imitations which have in various ways illuminated either the original text, our modern world, or both. They have written modern versions of

ORIGINAL

That time of year thou mayst in me behold
When yellow leaves, or none, or few, do hang
Upon those boughs which shake against the cold,
Bare ruined choirs, where late the sweet birds sang.
In me thou seest the twilight of such day
As after sunset fadeth in the west;
Which by and by black night doth take away,
Death's second self that seals up all in rest.
In me thou seest the glowing of such fire,
That on the ashes of his youth doth lie,
As the deathbed whereon it must expire,
Consumed with that which it was nourished by.
    This thou perceiv'st, which makes thy love more strong,
    To love that well, which thou must leave ere long. (879)

Shakespeare

PARODY

That time of year thou mayst in me behold
When yellow teeth, or none, or few do stay
In softened gums which chatter 'gainst the cold.
A halo of hair, yet sparse and bristly grey
In me thou seest, and yet thou failst to see
My heart, that hasn't changed inside.
Inside I'm more than how I look to thee.
My body's weak, but my soul shall never die.
In me thou seest what soon shall be thy fate.
My mind a mix of thoughts half done,
Cherished loves shriveled to bitter hate,
Awaiting friends who oft forget to come.
This thou perceiv'st, which keeps thee from my side,
And chokes thy love until the day I've died.

Melissa

ORIGINAL

THE GOOD MORROW

I wonder, by my troth, what thou and I
Did, till we loved? Were we not weaned till then,
But sucked on country pleasures, childishly?
Or snorted we in the seven sleepers' den?
'Twas so; but this, all pleasures fancies be.
If ever any beauty I did see,
Which I desired, and got, 'twas but a dream of thee.

133

And now good morrow to our waking souls,
Which watch not one another out of fear;
For love all love of other sights controls,
And makes one little world an everywhere.
Let sea discoverers to new worlds have gone,
Let maps to others, worlds on worlds have shown:
Let us possess one world; each hath one and is one.

My face in thine eye, thine in mine appears,
And true plain hearts do in the faces rest;
Where can we find two better hemispheres,
Without sharp North, without declining West?
Whatever dies was not mixed equally;
If our two loves be one, or thou and I
Love so alike that none do slacken, none can die. (1063)

Donne

PARODY

THE GOOD TORO

I wonder, by my blade, what thou and I
Did, till we cut? Had I no machine till then,
But cut country lawns, so primitively?
Or pushed and snipped I for neighborhood Men?
'Twas so; but then, Sears' catalog was sent me.
If ever any mower I did see,
Which I desired, and got, 'twas but a dream of thee.

And now good Toro you do soothe my soul,
Saving me the pains of my old John Deere;
No strain in adjusting your controls,
Cutting with ease all weeds and grass everywhere.
Let some others new fangled tractors own,
Let others believe advertisements shown:
Let only us, by mowing in truth, stand alone.

For this device is more than it appears,
Markedly superior to the rest,
Going beyond grass, for both hemispheres,
Blowing snow in the North, leaves in the West.
What lawn may die was not mowed properly;
With sun and rain, or my Toro and I
With the gifts of nature and machine, none can die.

Peter

Old English riddles, dramatic monologues imagined to have been spoken by Beowulf, and a "boasting speech" by Mohammed Ali in the style of an Anglo-Saxon hero, all following the conventions of Old English poetry. Several students in my Chaucer courses have written imitations of "The General Prologue" to *The Canterbury Tales,* usually in iambic pentameter couplets, sometimes even attempting to use Chaucer's Middle English.

If you do attempt a parody of this sort, try to be as faithful as you can to the style of the original. Show your reader how thoroughly you have interiorized its poetic conventions and "intellectual tics." At its best, writing of this sort is not only elegant and fun, but incisive literary criticism: you teach your reader to see the work, at least the parts you parody, as you do. Mohammed Ali's boast, for example, even while it showed a familiarity with the forms and conventions of Old English poetry, suggested something about the survival in an analogous modern context of the Anglo-Saxon warrior's spirit of assertiveness on the brink of battle. Two different students wrote mock cantos of Dante's *Comedy.* In his work, Dante's journey presents a "moral geography" of hell, purgatory, and paradise: a soul's location in the afterlife defines the moral values by which the person lived. In their cantos, both students imagined a person on a later journey through the otherworld, there encountering Dante's own spirit. One student found Dante in hell among the Blasphemers; the other in Purgatory among the Proud. In both cases he was being punished for his arrogance in presuming to pass judgment upon the lives of his contemporaries. What made the students' poems so successful was the way they imitated Dante's stylistic and conceptual habits: filled with telling allusions to various different parts of the *Comedy,* they could have been written only by people who had assimilated Dante's poem in great detail and with great sensitivity. Parodies, by the way, are very often acts of love; people rarely devote this much time and effort to a work that is not worth it.

Imitation of Modern Literary or Cultural Forms

I have also had students devise modern alternates to Chaucer's "General Prologue" as a means for presenting characters in a quasi-encyclopedic format. One wrote about arriving in Canterbury with Chaucer's group of Pilgrims in the style of an article for *The New York Times* travel section. Another wrote a mock yearbook with invented biographies, student activities, and quotations, imagining for each pilgrim the high school characteristics that would develop into the characters as we have them. In both cases, the fun and value came from the writer's ability to invent specific details which recalled and reacted to details from Chaucer's text. The intent was not to escape from, but rather to illuminate, the literary work dealt with. One student imagined the sexually aggressive Wife of Bath on a television talk show; another, in a *Playboy* interview. Another dealt with

"The Clerk's Tale," in which the improbably patient Griselda endures one affront after another from her increasingly obsessive husband, as an episode in the soap opera "Patience Place."

Finally, several students have written modern variants of Chaucer's *Troilus and Criseyde,* a romance about two young lovers in the doomed city of ancient Troy. Jennifer rewrote the story as a modern "romance" of the type you'd find on the shelves near the supermarket checkout, beginning her version as follows:

> The tall and glamorous Criseyde glided into the fashionable hall, located in the exciting Greenwich Village section of New York City. Her flowing black gown enhanced the shimmering clear blue of her electric eyes. She slid into an elegant mahogany chair, the color of which contrasted darkly with her golden tresses. Crossing her shapely legs, she glanced across the *Palladium,* the most popular club in the Big Apple. Criseyde, the young and beautiful widow, glistened like a brilliant diamond among rough stones. . . .

In Chaucer's romance, the Palladion is the name of the annual celebration of Pallas Athena, goddess of Wisdom, at which Troilus first sees Criseyde and falls in love with her. In reconceiving the encounter as taking place in a singles bar, and the form as the modern "romance" of soft-core sexploitation, Jennifer is able to suggest something about the diminution of the term "romance" in our own culture, while simultaneously suggesting a sinister dimension to what is going on in Chaucer's poem as well.

Greg's response to the *Troilus* was a made-for-television movie called "Trevor and Chrissie" as seen through the eager eyes of Randall, Jr., an eleven-year-old who "has seen previews for it throughout the week and also read the *TV Guide* review that called it 'a hot and steamy romance.'" What Greg presents is an indirect commentary on Chaucer's use of an intrusive narrator who interrupts his story, particularly at moments of sexual interest, in a way that breaks the emotional spell he is creating. In the following passage, Greg is approaching his conclusion:

> Chrissie rolls her black silk stocking off of her well-formed calves. Trevor kisses her neck. "I'm crazy about you!" he says. He kisses her shoulder and reaches for the tassled silk strap that holds on her nightgown. He begins to pull it below her shoulder. Randall, Jr., has stopped breathing. He sits trembling, his eyes focused on the screen. Trevor pulls the strap even lower and starts on the other. Chrissie arches her back and licks her lips.
>
> The screen goes blank for a half second.
>
> "NEW CHEESE WIZ, NOW IN MICROWAVABLE CONTAINER!"

The intrusion of the commercial and the eleven-year-old's voyeurism both create effects very much analogous to those of the *Troilus*'s narrator. As such, the parody is itself an act of interpretive analysis.

Rewriting the Text

You might rewrite a passage from a piece of fiction from an alternative point of view. If it is written in the third person, for example, rewrite it as if it were narrated by one of the characters. This would require you to be confident about the limits of the character's knowledge and about the peculiar qualities that would affect how this character would serve as a filter or center of consciousness through which the story could be told. You might also rewrite a work in a different genre: if it's a narrative, rewrite it as dialogue; if it's a play, retell it through a narrator. With any of these topics, what you would probably discover and should be sure to demonstrate is the way in which fundamental artistic choices limit subsequent decisions and predetermine the range of esthetic effects.

Rewriting the Ending

One day last semester, a student came up to me after class and said in an offhanded way, "You know, I really don't like the way *Sir Gawain and the Green Knight* ends." I was a bit distracted at the time and let the remark pass. Only later did I realize that I'd missed an opportunity. I should have said, "If you don't like the ending, rewrite it." The student would then have had to engage questions of structure, of theme, of closure. In order to figure out why he didn't like the ending, he'd first have had to figure out very carefully just why the poem *does* end as it does and how that ending affects him. Next time I'll be ready!

Creating Dialogues

One way to demonstrate your mastery of the subject matter in a course is to create imagined discussions. For example, imagine an encounter between two or more of the writers whose works you're reading in a course. Or between two or more characters, perhaps from different works. Or between a writer and one or more of his or her characters.

Some Final Examples

For her paper on *Troilus and Criseyde,* Lisa wrote an imagined letter from Criseyde to Helen of Troy, composed after the fall of the city when she and Helen are both safely back in Greece, in which she presents her side of the story which Chaucer tells. Since Helen puts in a cameo appearance in Chaucer's romance, Lisa's premise is not really far-fetched, especially since Troilus and Criseyde exchange letters both before they become lovers and after they are separated, and these letters become one of the ways in which Chaucer himself presents their characters. Lisa's letter, in fact, filled with specific references to episodes in Chaucer's romance all as perceived by Criseyde, is really a creative variant of the traditional paper analyzing a character.

I'll end with two more examples from the survey course. One student transformed the quarreling of Adam and Eve, a moment of epic grandeur in Book IX of *Paradise Lost,* into a dispute among the actors on the set of the fictional soap opera, "Paradise Tossed." In this imagined dialogue, the actress, Eve, was protesting the role which the creator (presumably God) and the writer of the series (Milton) had conspired for her to play. Another student wrote a poem in blank verse, imitating Milton's form, with the capitalized first words of each line forming an acrostic, spelling out vertically down the left margin the words "OF PARADISE LOST AND RE-GAINED." (We had seen Milton use this technique on one occasion in his poem.) The subject matter of the student's poem, however, was not adapted from Milton, but from Chaucer: it imagined the emotional reaction of the maiden who is raped in the initial episode of "The Wife of Bath's Tale." Either of these students might have written about the cultural basis of gender roles or about the cultural distortion inherent in the canon of exclusively male-authored texts enshrined in the traditional *Beowulf* to 1800 survey course. In a way, both did.

□

The Experimental Tradition

If some of the student papers I've been discussing in this chapter seem too experimental to you, I would suggest that they are in many ways similar to works we normally think of as "great" literature. When works become accepted as influential or significant within our cultural tradition, it is easy for us to forget that often they were originally daring. Perhaps you have recognized this playful quality in some of the works I've mentioned already in this chapter: Swift's "Modest Proposal" and *Gulliver's Travels* and Donne's "The Bait" come readily to mind. But did you think of how outrageous Dante was in the *Comedy* in claiming that he's telling us about a journey he took through hell, purgatory, and heaven, conducted at first by the ancient Roman poet Virgil, then by a woman he had once loved, and finally by St. Bernard? Does Chaucer's conceptual daring occur to you when he insists that he was only a reporter traveling on the pilgrimage to Canterbury Cathedral, thereby denying authorial responsibility for the tales he narrates? His lesser known *Troilus and Criseyde* is equally daring in its insistence that the narrator is a pedantic scholar, innocent of sexual intimacy, who is translating from Latin into English a lost history of the Trojan War at the center of which is a story of passionate love. When the story he is translating turns erotic, he becomes alternately flustered and voyeuristic; when it turns tragic, he feels dread at his obligation to be true to a "history" he can't alter.

What all these texts share is their fundamental "bookishness." They are incorporating, reacting against, even rewriting earlier works from the culture in which they share, and in so doing they are contributing to a tradition which goes back to antiquity. The first-century Roman poet Ovid, in his *Heroides,* wrote a series of fictional letters, supposedly written by famous heroines, in which they were presenting revisionist versions of the stories about them which literary tradition had perpetuated. As we get closer to our own time, we sometimes lose sight of the fact that authors are reworking the literary past. Mark Twain, for example, is so much of an American institution as a humorist that we might overlook his brilliance in putting his Connecticut Yankee into King Arthur's court, thereby inter-secting the worlds of modern scientific skepticism and medieval magic, the traditional concepts of military courtesy and chivalry found in Arthurian romance and the technological horrors of American Civil War weapons. In our own time, John Gardner's novel *Grendel* presents a book-long stream-of-consciousness monologue of the thoughts of the monster from *Beowulf.* Grendel's mind is filled with specific echoes from the Anglo-Saxon epic as re-imagined from his point of view, but the book's real focus seems to be to provide a commentary on certain twentieth-century philosophical and political ideologies to which the monster's ideas bear a disquieting similarity.

What all of these writers are doing is playing with and interpreting the inherited literary tradition, while finding ways to let it speak to their own worlds. There are times when you might choose to do the same. In fairness to you and your teachers, however, I have to conclude by reminding you that the kind of paper I've been talking about is not always appropriate. It's important for you to ascertain whether such an approach would be acceptable before submitting such a paper. Nevertheless, if you're keeping a course-related journal, either as a requirement or on your own, it would be perfectly natural for you to explore this kind of writing there. More-over, remember that writing about literature need not always be a com-mand performance and that your teacher need not be your only audience. Why not write something like this to show to your friends? And if the paper works, consider showing it to your teacher even if it doesn't count as part of a grade. Writing for an audience rather than for a grade might be an important step in your development as a writer.

As a teacher, when I approach a stack of student papers, I want to be taught. As a result of your paper, I want to read the work you're writing about in a new way. The kind of paper I've been discussing in this chapter can have the effect of "de-familiarizing" a work of literature. Works that were startling when they were originally written—and startling for me when I originally read them—can come to seem normal, tame, familiar, after they've been processed through the forms and formulas of academia year after year. Your paper can help make the work's original lightning visible, both for you and for me. Finally, it can help you incorporate those works into your own consciousness—of yourself, your literary tradition, and your world—in a playful way, and for those of us who love literature, our tradition can appropriately be considered our playground.

□

Works Cited

Donne, John. "The Bait" and "The Good Morrow." *The Norton Anthology of English Literature.* Gen. Ed. M. H. Abrams. 5th ed. New York: Norton, 1986.

Marlowe, Christopher. "The Passionate Shepherd to His Love." *The Norton Anthology of English Literature.* Gen. Ed. M. H. Abrams. 5th ed. New York: Norton, 1986.

Ralegh, Walter. "The Nymph's Reply to the Shepherd." *The Norton Anthology of English Literature.* Gen. Ed. M. H. Abrams. 5th ed. New York: Norton, 1986.

Shakespeare, William. "That Time of Year Thou Mayst in Me Behold." *The Norton Anthology of English Literature.* Gen. Ed. M. H. Abrams. 5th ed. New York: Norton, 1986.

CHAPTER 9

Examining the Essay Examination

Tony Magistrale

P lease write on two of the following topics. You will have 50 minutes to complete this examination. Write only in the examination book provided.

1.   Define Wordsworth's attitude toward childhood as it is expressed in *The Prelude.* (25 minutes)

2.   Discuss the importance of the city in two of Dostoevski's novels. (25 minutes)

3.   Compare Emily Dickinson's view on immortality in the poem "I've known a Heaven, like a Tent" to her perspective on this subject in any of her other poems studied this semester. (25 minutes)

When I showed these exam topics to several of the authors of the other chapters in this book, each one gave me a similar response: relief at not having to answer any of the questions. If English professors are glad to be free of such an ordeal, why do they put their students through it? Is the essay examination an educational rite of passage? A testing routine teachers are reluctant to give up? A fundamental illustration of the profession's tendency toward sadistic behavior? Maybe a little of each. But it is also something more.

Sid Poger, author of the poetry chapter, told me that he assigns essay examinations out of a desire to "help the student discover for him or her self the major theme of the course throughout the term. That idea is what the essay will address, and I hope the student who has been in class, in mind as well as body, will come to recognize what's been going on." Another colleague, Tom Simone, feels that an essay exam is "the place for a student to shine. If he or she has been paying attention and has been thinking about the class material, my essays are always open-ended enough to allow him or her to show off." Bill Stephany, our medievalist, reminded me that he looks for "connections that surprise the teacher . . . giving information on topics I want to know more about." Editor Toby Fulwiler often sees essay exams as "more like 'free writes' than methodically structured prose."

If you look carefully at the reasons each of these professors gives for assigning essay questions, it is clear that exams are always more than a means for establishing a grade. Each of these teachers seeks to test your ability to interpret aspects of specific literary works or to synthesize disparate material covered in class into a more comprehensive whole. Sometimes, as in the Dickinson question above, a writing task may also ask you to recognize similarities and differences between two or more characters, themes, symbols, or individual texts. In any event, your instructor is interested not only in how much you know about a particular subject, but also about the course as a whole.

In a very real way, you begin to prepare for an exam on the first day of class, as you notice your professor's assignments, biases, and perspectives. Since essays are usually written for an audience of one—your teacher—what you say on an exam might be viewed as an intellectual dialogue with a person you know quite well. This doesn't mean that your writing should get chummy or informal, but it does suggest that you pay attention to your professor's beliefs. If you intend to present an opinion or perspective that will run contrary to your teacher's, be prepared to back it up especially well. In other words, be aware of your instructor's position and clearly acknowledge this awareness somewhere in the essay. Then go ahead and strike out on your own. Remember Professor Stephany's request for "surprises." You won't surprise any professor by writing safe answers, by simply reiterating interpretations from a lecture. On any given essay examination, I expect at least half the answers to do this, and quite frankly, after reading thirty attempts to reconstruct my lectures, it is always refreshing to discover someone saying something unique—especially if it is an articulate and supported reassessment of my interpretation.

But be careful here. Exam surprises can be both good and bad. The kind of surprise Bill Stephany encourages gets a teacher excited about what you have to say; it demonstrates not only a solid understanding of a poem or a novel, but also shows that you have spent some time considering its larger connections to the course and to your own life. In contrast, a student who disagrees with me without much thought and merely for the sake of saying something different or who goes off into a new interpretation without adequate support for the position is surely going to give me a surprise, but it will be one I will probably not enjoy.

□

Writing Under Pressure

Composing answers to an essay examination may appear difficult enough when you are given several days to construct responses. The assignment becomes all the more challenging, however, when you must write in a short, predetermined period of time, usually surrounded by other students who seem to possess magical pens that seldom rise from the exam book's page. Writing under a time restraint demands even more concision and discipline than ordinarily employed in producing a research paper or a critical essay over an extended period of days or weeks. Time restraints preclude the luxury of multiple drafts or the leisure of returning to the work after an elapsed length of time. Perhaps this is one reason why so many teachers continue to assign in-class essay exams and believe they are important; as is often the case in contexts outside the classroom, we do not always have the opportunity to polish language until it says exactly what we want it to. We are often required to think quickly, to use words spontaneously yet accurately. And although this is a difficult activity, there are a few tricks you might learn.

One of the most common (and natural) reactions to an hour essay exam is panic. My own students reminded me of the anxiety and tension associated with this type of writing when I asked them to list their own attitudes toward the experience: "sweating palms, faint nausea," "a mixture of excitement and apprehension," "a pressing urge to go to the bathroom," and "a desire to hurry up and start the exam in order to get it over with."

On the typical examination, you have about twenty or thirty minutes per essay, so there is little room for mistakes. Your answers must get to the point immediately and concisely. You can't easily cross out or start over. Therefore, you must compose essays which are clearly written and, most important, carefully organized to answer the question being asked. But before considering a general procedure for structuring answers to essay questions, let's consider a few fundamental points to keep in mind prior to the actual writing.

Preliminary Steps and Some Practical Advice

An essay exam is first and foremost an essay. As such, it is important to decide what to include, what to exclude, how to arrange, and what to emphasize.

1. Before beginning any writing, you should read the entire test. What choices, if any, does the exam allow? What specific kinds of information does each essay require?

2. Which of the questions do you feel most comfortable answering (it might help to start with the easiest and work your way to the most difficult)?

3. Allot yourself a certain period of time per answer and hold yourself to it. Instructors seldom sympathize with an indication you have run out of time.

4. Plan on building in enough time to read the exam over before handing it in. Simple qualifications to central arguments as well as mistakes in diction are hard to recognize in a first draft, but may be captured in revision.

5. Finally, when you feel ready to begin the actual writing, keep the following points in mind to help in organizing and presenting the essay: (a) circle core issues, concepts, and requests in the exam question itself; (b) use frequent paragraph breaks. Each new paragraph is the place to make new arguments to recapture a tired professor's attention; (c) leave space on the left side of your paper or exam book for second thoughts and revisions; (d) write on every other line, as this will make it easier for your professor to read and for you to make changes directly into the text of your answer.

Types of Information Requests

The key to performing well on an essay examination is to understand completely what the questions are asking. The language of a given assignment will often contain hidden clues which reveal directions toward composing a potential answer. Consider, for example, this examination question from a recent American literature midterm:

The general tone of Crevecoeur's Letters of an American Farmer presents an image of America that finds restatement in the work of Emerson and the transcendentalists: it is that of a young, beautiful, optimistic, and enduring country which is destined to complete the cycle of history begun in Europe. Compare this version of America to that found in Twain's *Huckleberry Finn*.

First, notice how much information is already supplied in the topic itself: an implied chronology, that Emerson and the transcendentalists are coming out of an American literary tradition that was shaped by earlier writers such as Crevecoeur. Moreover, the exam also supplies you with a solid definition of what Crevecoeur and the transcendentalists generally felt about America. Lastly, the topic also suggests that this version of America must be compared or contrasted with Twain's perception. These are your starting points, and perhaps the easiest way to begin composing a response would be to assemble evidence from *Huckleberry Finn* that either agrees or disagrees with the Crevecoeur-transcendentalist position.

However, it is quite possible to argue that Twain's novel presents at the same time *both* a negative portrait of America's social institutions and a positive example of American individualism in the survivalist instincts of Huck. Another way to answer this question, then, would be to refrain from making the distinction regarding whether *Huck Finn* is essentially an optimistic or pessimistic work, but instead to demonstrate where the novel both disagrees and concurs with the perspective associated with Crevecoeur and the transcendentalists. The word "compare" in the exam question allows you this flexibility. The term "comparison" usually means a larger, more inclusive approach to the topic that may include both similarities and differences. But if you were asked instead to *contrast* Twain's book with these earlier writers, you would want to emphasize the differences only. Therefore, any question that asks you to compare or contrast may be requesting (1) the differences between two or more things, (2) the similarities between generally dissimilar things, (3) an explanation of one thing in relation to something else, (4) a basis for evaluation and/or argument. All comparisons and contrasts require you to go beyond individual positions, theses, or texts—to think about the *interrelationships* between characteristics of two or more concepts.

If an essay examination does not request some type of a comparison or contrast between individual works or concepts, it will generally ask you to *analyze* a single literary text, or some aspect of it.

1. What is the significance of Orlick's relationship to Pip in Dickens' *Great Expectations?*
2. Discuss the symbolic function of the peacock in Flannery O'Connor's novella *The Displaced Person.*

Both questions ask you to explain the relationship between parts and a larger whole. By first identifying and then explaining the significance of a literary text's components—considering what, where, why, and how they operate—we gain a fuller appreciation of how individual elements work together to produce structural unity. To understand Orlick's connection to Pip, you must first establish that Orlick is a reflection of one dimension of Pip's larger personality—a representation of the latter's darkest impulses. It is really quite unnecessary to delve into the "other sides" of Pip's complex character to answer this question; in fact, pursuing them may distract your reader from the real purpose of the writing and thus weaken your analysis. The exam requests only information about where Pip and Orlick share mutual correspondences, and this should remain the focus of your entire essay.

Planning

Once you understand the type of information the exam question requests, you should plan a response to it. First, make a simple list of main ideas. This will generate new concepts at the same time as it will help in formulating the language you will need to construct a coherent argument. Second, use a written plan to keep your writing focused on the subject. After you have composed such a plan, check it against the examination request. Are the topics you intend to discuss in your answer relevant to what is being asked? Here is an outline Nancy used to help her address the midterm examination question raised at the beginning of this chapter, "Compare Emily Dickinson's view on immortality in the poem 'I've known a Heaven, like a Tent' to her perspective on this subject in any one of her other poems studied this semester." Nancy's American literature class had not studied this poem prior to the exam, so it was reproduced under the topic assignment.

NANCY'S PLAN

INTERPRET POEM: —"heaven" as circus tent
                     —circus tent as symbol of afterlife

COMPARE TO: "I heard a Fly buzz—when I died"
                 —human isolation
                 —lost vision, taken away
                 —same conclusion: no hope/light

Looking at Nancy's plan, it becomes clear that she has constructed an excellent framework for composing an essay answer. She chooses first to analyze the poem cited in the exam, "I've known a Heaven, like a Tent," emphasizing the use of a departed circus as a metaphor for describing the loss of heaven. (Pay particular attention to the manner in which she will blend her reading of the poem with specific excerpts from the poem itself, thereby making her interpretation all the more persuasive.) From there, she then seeks to complete the assignment by comparing it to another Dickinson poem, "I heard a Fly buzz." Because the exam asked for a comparison,

Nancy elected to work with a poem that has a perspective similar to "I've known a Heaven, like a Tent." She could just as well have gone in the opposite direction, choosing a poem to contrast with the exam selection. Finally, notice that in both the plan and the essay that emerge, Nancy maintains her critical attention on the unifying thesis of the issue at hand: how each of these poems reflects a comparable attitude toward the theme of immortality.

> In the poem "I've known a Heaven, like a Tent," Emily Dickinson in her own way is describing her idea of heaven. It seems as though she breaks a childhood myth with this poem. The myth being that heaven is a visible place that awaits us with its great pearly gates and its angels waiting to take you in and check your name off this great ledger that some old white-haired man is seated in front of. This "Heaven" she has "known," may refer to a glimpse of God's happy place, or perhaps she is recalling a special "heavenly" moment or event that profoundly touched her life. In either event, myth or reality, this recollected image of heaven is now gone, and it is significant that she ties its departure to a circus show "That dazzled, Yesterday." The carnival is a visual image from childhood (perhaps invoking the poet's earlier, innocent perception of heaven?) that promises fun and excitement, but in this poem those promises are unfulfilled, as the tent "wrap[s] its shining Yards—/Pluck[s] up its stakes, and disappear[s]—." What was here yesterday, her heaven or hope of attaining this place, has gone without a figment or trace—utterly dissolved and "Then swallowed up, of View."
>
> Dickinson now interprets heaven as a vast emptiness, just a "View." She discovers that heaven cannot be traced with empirical evidence, that it is just an eternity: "No Trace—no Figment of the Thing," leaving only "just the miles of Stare." This theme of disillusionment with heaven, of eternal loneliness and emptiness, can be traced throughout her poetry.
>
> In "I heard a Fly buzz—when I died," when the speaker began the poem in the process of dying, she rose above herself and was aware of *everything* going on around her: the "Breaths gathering firm," the "Eyes wrung dry," and the "Keepsakes—Signed away." But when she finally dies—at the moment of death—"the windows failed—and then/ I could not see to see," meaning that she could no longer see anything ahead of her. Just as in the exam poem, the afterlife portrayed in "I heard a Fly buzz" is unattainable, the "Heaven" remains unseen, a mere suffocating darkness. As her "Heaven" in the circus poem just dissolves, in "I heard a Fly buzz" there is no hope

for a beautiful or fulfilling afterlife. Her view in
both these poems is filled with the dark despair of a
Melville or a Hawthorne, rather than the unqualified
faith in the future of a transcendentalist.

Nancy's analysis is a good illustration of how the act of writing helps
the mind not only to clarify concepts, but also to develop new insights and
parallels. Her answer is a study in the art of discovery. It starts by working
through the complex details of a poem she has never seen before and
concludes by reconnecting to information in "I heard a Fly buzz," which
is a work she knows quite well. Notice that in writing about both of these
poems Nancy not only discovers some similarities they share, but also goes
on to enlarge her understanding of Dickinson as a nineteenth-century
American poet.

The concluding sentence of her essay is different—in diction and
scope—from the rest of her response. Here is evidence of the "surprise"
Stephany mentioned earlier when explaining his reason for assigning essay
topics. Nancy's final sentence jumps at the reader because it extends her
analysis of these two Dickinson poems to include an important assertion
about the poet's relationship to her literary contemporaries. If Nancy were
able to revise this essay, or if it were a take-home examination, this final
sentence might well become her first sentence, as it is a large thesis statement that is supported in the act of interpreting the two poems. In any
event, as this concluding sentence represents the culmination of Nancy's
effort to understand the poetry of Emily Dickinson, she might highlight
it in a new paragraph or by somehow distinguishing it from the rest of the
essay.

□

Structuring Essay Answers

Under the tense and circumscribed conditions of a timed examination,
most students tend to write too much: by saying as much as they can about
a particular text or a writer, they trust that the torrent of information will
sufficiently impress the teacher or somehow manage to strike upon a
response relevant to the question. Consider, for example, Ken's response
to a midterm examination question asking him to discuss the significance
of Madeline Usher's role in Poe's tale "The Fall of the House of Usher":

Poe's tales have no apparent logic to them. He was a
writer from the period of dark romanticism and his stories often show a person's inability to control experiences that exist psychologically and from his personal
negative motivations. Poe hated women, or at least he
didn't trust them very far, so all his male characters

rebel against them. Poe's own relationship to women was
influenced by his mother's rejection of him at an early
age and he spent the rest of his life trying to find someone to take her place. The male characters in his stories
take drugs and use exotic settings to forget tragic love
affairs that are similar to the ones Poe himself experienced with women in his own life. For them, time is
always an enemy—it is there as a reminder of frustration
and ultimate death. Madeline Usher is a symbol of Poe's
women. She is all the things her brother hates, all the
things out of his control. She suffers from the same kind
of illness that is killing Usher.

What can we say is strong in this essay? Ken demonstrates a wide-
ranging understanding of Poe. Many of the points he makes in this essay
are valid. He knows, for instance, that Poe was a dark romantic, that the
writer's feelings toward women were ambivalent, that his male protago-
nists are deeply troubled individuals subject to compulsive and aberrant
behavior, that time is a symbol of human destruction throughout Poe's
stories, and finally, that Madeline is a constant source of irritation for her
brother. What are the problems with this essay? A central one is within
its organization or structure; Ken wanders around the subjects of Poe's
fiction in a manner painfully reminiscent of Roderick himself wandering
the corridors of the Usher mansion. His writing has neither direction nor
thesis; he never really comes to terms with Madeline's role in the story,
and thus produces more of a collection of assertions rather than a cohesive
essay. Instead of pursuing only material relevant to answering the exam
question, Ken tries to impart everything he knows about Poe's fiction. He
doesn't really begin to answer the question until line 14 of a 17-line
response.

There are several places in this answer where the writer might have
"turned the corner" to commence a more focused analysis of "The Fall of
the House of Usher," and Madeline's character specifically. What, for
instance, are "all the things her brother hates, all the things out of his
control"? If Madeline is symbolic of these restrictive elements, a more
detailed explanation of (1) exactly what these elements are and (2) how
they are embodied in Madeline would help the reader to see the connection
between her character and the rest of the story. Once Madeline's relationship to Roderick is ascertained and clarified, then a discussion of the larger
issue of Poe's general attitude toward women—either in other stories or
as biographical criticism—makes more sense. But unless these issues are
tied directly to the discussion of Madeline's relationship with her brother,
the examination question remains essentially unanswered. Rather than
simply "leaping into" an essay answer on an exam, and thereby encouraging your thoughts to wander in a number of directions, as in Ken's example
above, it is better to keep your writing focused. Here's where some sort
of writing plan can prove particularly useful, since long, meandering re-

sponses suggest imprecise, fuzzy thinking, even if relevant information is embedded somewhere in your response.

Once you have decided exactly what the exam question requires and the plan is completed, you are ready to begin writing. But how? Your written plan contains pertinent information for developing an essay, but in what order should these points be presented? What form should the answer take? What should come first?

In the comparison-contrast example Nancy supplied earlier, the writer saved the actual comparison until the end, after she had focused individual attention on each of the Dickinson poems. On the one hand, I think her essay is organized in such a way that the material is presented clearly and concisely (and organization is one of the most difficult accomplishments in writing an essay exam, since good insights may occur late in the writing). On the other hand, Nancy could have structured things differently and still achieved similar results. Employing the same ideas listed under her plan, the major points of the essay could easily be reorganized to introduce the comparison between the two poems at the beginning, rather than at the end.

In discussing strategies for structuring essay exams, several of my English department colleagues suggested that that strongest part of any essay should be its beginning. Since professors read hundreds of essays in a rush, students should give them what they want up front, and certainly within the first paragraph. Consequently, Nancy might have inverted the form of her essay—starting with a few sentences to introduce the most important points of comparison between the two poems, then a paragraph or two describing how each poem connects to the theme of immortality, and concluding with a summary that brings the two poems together again.

Nancy's writing illustrates that the form an essay takes is often less important than the information it provides and the degree to which that information responds accurately to what the examination question asks. Other instructors may feel differently. It would be well within the province of a teacher to argue that Nancy's answer does not confront the issue of an actual comparison between two of Dickinson's poems until the final paragraph, and as a consequence her response is not so complete as it should be. Some instructors might feel that since the request for a comparison is at the heart of the examination question, language directly addressing this issue should appear within the essay's opening paragraph.

Thus, the standard advice in structuring essays is to create some version of a "funnel" shape: start broadly by stating and defining the most important elements, or thesis, of your argument. Then, gradually narrow or specify your main argument through examples and illustrations of the points raised initially in the broad thesis statement. In this way, your examples and analyses will refer to concepts you have established, and your supporting evidence can be tailored to fit the major points which began the essay. This principle can be illustrated in the paragraphs that follow, taken from a midterm examination in which Susan was asked to relate the theme of Walt Whitman's short poem "A noiseless patient spider" to his larger poetic vision:

> Walt Whitman was a poet who wrote about the unity of all things. He took Emerson's doctrines to their furthest extremes, believing that not only were the diverse and individual elements of the universe related to one another but, in fact, that they were reflective of the same identical thing.
>
> Whitman's themes were about everything—a blade of grass, a prostitute, a dying man alone on a battlefield— and he believed sincerely that no one thing was better, or worse, than another. A spider (which before this class I would probably squash) is only a small part of the "whole," yet is still connected to the "whole," just as one human being is representative of a larger humanity.
>
> The spider is isolated, as are those individual men and women who fail to explore and learn from their surroundings and others, but the difference is that the spider creates a web which "connects" things together. Whitman's verse accomplishes the same sort of connecting. He unifies everything and everybody in poetic song. In the first half of "Song of Myself" the poet takes all of life's experiences and makes them his own—he observes and studies them—and then seeks to understand how they are connected to one another.
>
> In "A noiseless patient spider" he asks his soul the same question: "Where do I stand?/ Surrounded, detached, seeking spheres to connect them." Only by "connecting" himself to everything and everyone he observes can the poet, like the spider's web, "form a bridge" that will link him to the rest of the world.

In the opening paragraph, Susan begins her analysis with a broad assessment of Whitman's poetry; she even includes a mention of Emerson's influence on his work. After establishing the unity theme in Whitman's poetry, she ends her first paragraph by tying this concept to "A noiseless patient spider": "A spider (which before this class I would probably squash) is only a small part of the 'whole,' just as one human being is representative of a larger humanity."

In the second paragraph, Susan's analysis becomes more specific, centering on the relationship between the metaphor of the spider's web and Whitman's broader poetic principles: ". . . the spider creates a web which 'connects' things together. Whitman's verse accomplishes the same sort of connecting. He unifies everything and everybody in poetic song." The connection between "A noiseless patient spider" and Whitman's canon is made explicit in her reference to "Song of Myself," and here she is careful to stress common themes found in both poems. The use of the "funnel" structure as an organizing metaphor in this essay aids Susan in developing her argument in a systematic and coherent manner. As the answer unfolds, she gradually narrows her analysis from the general to the specific, so that by the conclusion Whitman's poetic vision and the symbolic spider web become synonymous in purpose: "Only by 'connecting' himself to everything and everyone he observes can the poet, like the spider's web, 'form the bridge' that will link him to the rest of the world."

□

Preparation for a Timed Essay Examination

Here's some good advice if you can follow it: A week or two before an examination, get together with several of your classmates and write three or four potential essay questions based upon lecture notes and textbook information. Compose answers to one or two of the questions posed by your classmates under exam conditions; allot the same amount of time your professor intends to allow. Once you have completed the essays, share your writing with the group, and suggest improvements for one another. This activity will help acquaint you with the process of having your work evaluated, at the same time as it will broaden your knowledge of the material in the course. You may even find yourself practicing an answer that will be similar (or, great joy, identical) to the very exam topic your professor poses.

□

The Take-Home Examination

A well-written essay—whether composed during a timed in-class examination or in response to a take-home assignment—reflects the strengths described in this chapter: it is organized and focused; it demonstrates the ability to analyze and/or engage comparative thought; it shows the capacity to assemble and assess information; and it indicates an understanding of course material and the capability to shape this understanding into writing appropriate to the exam topic. The take-home essay is closely related to its in-class brethren in form, content, and purpose. However, since they are each composed under different circumstances, there are some slight variations in their manner of production. Primarily, a take-home examination affords the chance to edit, to revise, and to rethink what you have composed. Furthermore, the take-home exam provides the opportunity to incorporate research—class notes, quotes, journals, and sometimes published scholarship—directly into the composition. It is, of course, a fatal mistake not to acknowledge citations used in a take-home exam. Richard Sweterlitsch, Jim Holstun, and Robyn Warhol provide assistance in their chapters for avoiding plagiarism, and their advice should be applied to take-home exams as well as to the composition of more formal research projects.

Using Class Notes and Journals

As Toby Fulwiler suggests in his chapter, journals are an excellent source for helping you to study for examinations, to assemble information for conducting research, and as a place to generate ideas through informal prose. Before writing a given essay assignment, read through your journal entries and class notes on areas germane to the topic. Sometimes you may discover whole sections or passages that require only slight modification for inclusion into the essay. Often a sentence or two, even the seed of an idea currently in undeveloped form, can point you in the direction for further writing.

Aside from generating ideas to use in composing a response, the journal is also the place to begin the actual writing of the essay itself. Since a take-home exam affords you a certain amount of flexible time, use the journal to freewrite about your subject. The journal will not only help to start the flow of writing itself, but a couple of good entries may become the basis for your essay.

Revising and Editing

Since the take-home examination typically allows you several days to produce an essay, the sooner you get started writing, the more chance you will have to polish and improve its contents. Once a first draft of the essay is complete, reread it from start to finish, paying particular attention to logic and overall organization. Is your thesis clear, and is it developed throughout the length of the essay? Does it answer the question? Do individual paragraphs fit together, or would the thesis be more coherent if the order of presentation were rearranged?

When the revisions are completed, read the work aloud to a friend before typing it. The very act of reading an essay aloud can often reveal places where language might be improved, or where the logic of the argument needs to be strengthened. I often dictate my own prose into a tape recorder; the act of hearing my thoughts forces me to concentrate on how the writing sounds—from the overall development of a thesis to the way in which individual words work (or do not work) harmoniously with one another.

Preparation for a Take-Home Essay Examination

A few days before the exam is distributed, spend a couple of hours marking passages in texts and journals that you consider significant. This activity will accomplish two things. First, it will refresh your memory by helping you to refocus material studied weeks ago. Second, like the outline plan described earlier in this chapter, these recollections will get you thinking about the most important aspects of a writer's canon. Instead of beginning the exam on the day you receive it, your preparation will place relevant information at your fingertips, giving you an obvious head start on assembling evidence. (This process is especially valuable prior to in-class open-book examinations. Premarked notations and quotes will save you precious minutes during the exam itself.)

☐

Beginning at the End: In Memory of Bells

Last year I returned to my undergraduate alma mater, Allegheny College, for the first time since graduation a decade earlier. I arrived on campus on a day late in May—one of those glorious spring afternoons filled with promise when even the earth of the western Pennsylvania snowbelt is refreshed in light. It was warm and final examinations were in session, so all the windows of Arter Hall, home of the English Department, were open to the afternoon. As I strolled alongside the building, bemused by the torrent of recollections each step seemed to summon, a series of bells sounded from inside indicating the start of a final exam. All the old feelings returned—the nervous fingers, the twitch somewhere near the base of my stomach. The exam bell removed the brightness of that May afternoon. I was back in the dim grey air of Arter Hall, blue book open on the desk in front of me, three exam topics measuring the distance between my pen and summer vacation. I may well have decided at that very moment to write the chapter you have just finished reading.

CHAPTER 10

Writing Research

Richard
Sweterlitsch

L ast spring in my American Literature course, I assigned a paper that
was to draw upon research. To most of the students, this meant
"research paper," and off they went to the library to look through the
card catalogue. One student, Marsha, remembered that her high school
teacher talked about how much Fitzgerald's relationship with Zelda affected *The Great Gatsby*. So she checked out Arthur Mizener's *The Far Side
of Paradise,* Sara Mayfield's *Exiles from Paradise: Zelda and F. Scott Fitzgerald,* and
Zelda: A Biography by Nancy Milford. She skimmed the first chapters of each
book and found enough material about the stormy relationship to fill a
dozen or so index cards. She returned to her room and spent an afternoon
arranging her notes; these she connected into a flowing essay, linked by
her own transitions. The next day she added her endnotes and a bibliography, making sure that all the correct forms were followed. Her work was
simple, to the point, and a waste of time.

Writing a paper based on research is nothing new for most students.
Somewhere in high school or college, everyone has written a research

paper, and many do what Marsha did. They scour the library card catalogue, find a couple of books and magazine articles related to their topic,
and skim through them, taking down some notes. Writing the paper means
piecing together quotes from various sources, writing footnotes and bibliography correctly, and turning in the paper for a grade. This is not research
writing.

Ken Macrorie in his book *Searching Writing* complains: "Most research
papers written in high school and college are bad jokes. They're funny
because they pretend to be so much and actually are so little" (116).
Marsha's paper had nothing to offer other than a demonstration of her
ability to stitch together a patchwork from diverse sources. While she took
a stab at researching a particular topic, she went no further than reproducing ideas from other scholars. Her voice was not heard; there was no sense
of personal excitement over researching some curiosity she had about the
novel. The paper offered no new insights and had no fresh purpose. Her
research, sketchy as it was, reinforced something she already knew, but she
had nothing new to share with me or anyone else in the class. It was all
so very little.

That the research paper has become "a bad joke" can't be blamed
completely on students, or on the instruction they received in high school.
Although literary scholars, who are often college professors as well, publish numerous articles and books based on their research, undergraduate
English majors who are aspiring to become members of the community of
scholars are not asked to write essays solidly grounded in research.

Writing up one's research is not a mindless task of regurgitating critics'
opinions. It is personal writing. The voice of the writer—the "I"—should
come through loudly and clearly. The "I think" and "I believe" have a
place in the research paper. Too often, research writing degenerates into
an impersonal treatise with no sense of the personal curiosity that
prompted the search in the first place or the personal excitement the
writers felt when they resolved their questions. The very personal critical
writings that characterize much of the literary criticism and research writings in the early nineteenth and early twentieth centuries have been replaced by the disinterested and sterile—and too often boring—voice of the
clinician, as literary scholars try to sound like something they are not—
scientists.

Research writing is not putting together divergent sources into a unified paper. Nor is it a mindless activity whose chief goal is to submit a
"correct" paper—that is, one in which the sources are correctly quoted,
noted, and enumerated in a bibliography, all according to the latest formula. Writing an intelligent, perceptive research paper marks the culmination of a personal inquiry into something that started out as a nagging
curiosity. Research writing ought to produce a good piece of writing that,
in turn, produces pleasure for author and readers.

After all, literary research is a type of humanistic inquiry. It is not an alienating experience, because research requires learning to network with the scholarly community for the purpose of gathering and eventually sharing information. Researchers become thinkers by taking their findings and synthesizing them with their own ideas in order to produce new knowledge, and they become writers when they present their findings in essays to the scholarly community. Writing based on research reinforces a symbiotic relationship between acquiring information and sharing new insights, between a literary scholar and the other members of the scholarly community. The literature class is one forum within the scholarly community where ideas about literature are shared among people with a common interest.

This book explains and examines a number of different approaches to writing about literature. Research is handmaid to many of them. A critical essay may receive a sharper edge when the writer has listened to the voice of other writers. The analytic paper may draw upon the insights other critics presented in published essays. But we should not think that the only reason for undertaking research is to write a critical, analytic paper. Novelists, poets, and playwrights undertake research to provide themselves with insights and details they want to use in their work. Shakespeare turned to Plutarch's *Lives* and Holinshed's *Chronicles* for situations, themes, and ideas. Norman Mailer's *Executioner's Song,* Capote's *In Cold Blood,* both drew heavily upon interviews. Several years ago, a colleague who was writing a novel asked me—a folklorist by training—for some information about an Irish custom related to horses. I gave him a copy of *Irish Folk Ways* by E. Estyn Evans. My colleague wanted to be sure he had presented a particular tradition in his novel accurately. All conscientious writers want to know that their allusions are accurate, and so they research them carefully before finally integrating them into their writing.

Whether one is writing an analytical paper, a play, a poem, short story, novel, or book review, knowing how to do effective research is an important skill. It is fitting that research and writing based on research be an integral part of every class. In this chapter, I emphasize the kind of research one undertakes in order to write critical and analytic papers, the kinds generally discussed in this book.

□

Getting Started

Writing a paper based primarily on research is different from other types of literary writing, but it does share some of the concerns of critical writing. In her chapter, Robyn Warhol points to the three main goals of critical writing: to describe, to evaluate, and to interpret a text. Research writing may have these same goals and others, but the writers of the research paper turn to a network of scholars and draw upon what they have to offer so that their own observations can be informed by a scholarly tradition.

The primary task with literary research is finding a subject to write about and then narrowing it down to a topic and then a thesis. As students of literature, we have one advantage: we usually have a specific text to deal with. Obviously knowing the text well is a good place to start, asking questions of and about the text sets up a dialogue, as it were, between the writer and the text. Read the text looking for something that strikes you. Jot down questions and notes to yourself as you read, either in a journal, or as I usually do, right on the text itself. Give your ideas free rein; let them float around in your head for a while. Do some free writing.

The questions you may ask are as endless as there are ways of answering them. For example, literary scholarship has gathered about itself a number of modes of inquiry. Historical questions can be asked about a text:

- □ When was it written?

- □ Under what circumstances was it written?

- □ What impact did it have on literature when it first appeared? On later writers?

- □ Are there different versions of a text and what significance do the variations have on the reading of a text?

Students of literature are also concerned with sources and analogues that influence writers and their works:

- □ What sources influenced a work or an author?

- □ How did the source influence the author?

- □ Why is one work in a particular period similar to or different from others in the same genre?

- □ Was an author familiar with a particular piece of literature?

Researchers very often go beyond a work and look for psychological, historical, cultural, and environmental factors that affected authors and their works, at the time they were first published and afterward.

- □ Are there autobiographical motifs in a work?

- □ Is the text based on historical fact?

- □ What ethnic and social concerns does the work raise?

The secret is to take something that you know very little about. Don't do what Marsha did when she wrote about Fitzgerald and Zelda. She knew what she was going to write even before she began her research and looked only for answers that suited the question she was asking.

Finding an Overview

When first approaching a potential topic, many researchers often turn to an encyclopedia or similar broad study. These resources lack the detail the serious researcher needs, but they are useful places to begin researching a problem. Among the more useful for the student of literature are Margaret Drabble's *The Oxford Companion to English Literature* (5th ed. New York: Oxford UP, 1985) and James D. Hart's *The Oxford Companion to American Literature* (5th ed. New York: Oxford UP, 1983). Two older general studies which weaned a number of scholars are Albert Baugh's *A Literary History of England* (2nd ed. Englewood Cliffs, NJ: Prentice-Hall, 1967) and Robert Spiller's *Literary History of the United States* (4th ed. New York: Macmillan, 1974). The *Oxford History of English Literature* series, begun in 1945, is very helpful because each volume is written by a specialist and each provides an excellent overview of literary periods and their major authors. Each book also has an important bibliography, albeit somewhat dated.

Of course, don't overlook introductions and notes in lit textbooks. For example, the Perkins, Bradley, Beatty, and Long two-volume anthology *The American Tradition in Literature* (6th ed. New York: Random House, 1985) not only provides broad introductions to various periods in American literature, but also offers biographical sketches of authors and a basic bibliography of some of the major primary and secondary sources. For English literature, you might consider *The North Anthology of English Literature* (5th ed. 2 vols. New York: Norton, 1986), under the general editorship of M. H. Abrams.

The purpose of your research at this stage is essentially exploratory: What have others to say about the topic I'm interested in pursuing? Perhaps you will discover that one of these studies will satisfy your curiosity and you won't want to pursue it any further. In any case, if these sources have something to say which you think is worth saving, make a note of the information and be sure to indicate to yourself exactly where you found it. You may want to return to it later.

At this stage too, don't forget your teacher and classmates. Research on a government project might need to be kept secret, but in literary circles, secrecy is often the bane of successful research. Your teacher might have some information to share with you or maybe some advice about where you can turn for information. Classmates are often thinking along the same lines. In their research they might come up with a lead worth following.

Following Leads

A couple of years ago, I assigned a research paper on any work by Faulkner. Tom, a junior majoring in English, liked *As I Lay Dying*. In particular, he was curious about Darl. Tom had taken Psychology 1, and he remembered that schizophrenia was discussed in the course. From what Tom could recall, Darl seemed to exhibit some of the symptoms. First Tom put up a trial balloon: in class, he asked me what I thought. Frankly, I liked the idea, but I couldn't offer much help other than suggesting he look in one of the Faulkner bibliographies to see what has been written about Darl. Some of the others in class agreed with Tom's ideas about Darl; others didn't, saying that Darl was probably the most sane of the whole Bundren clan. So Tom began some formal research.

He went first to his former psychology professor, who suggested an essay for Tom to read. That article whetted his curiosity even further. He was sure he was on to something, but he knew he needed to undertake some additional research. He looked through a Faulkner bibliography, which turned up a couple of useful articles, and he interviewed a social worker at a local mental health center. Armed with a much better understanding of what the mental illness was and what its outward signs were, Tom was prepared to analyze Darl and write the paper. The central thesis of the paper was Tom's—Darl was a schizophrenic—and his argument was his own, but it was buoyed by divergent critical opinions and information he gathered from the professionals.

Three summers ago, when I was teaching a course on Vermont literature, Martha, a sophomore, decided to research the background of "Marjorie Grey," a poem by a nineteenth-century Vermont local-color writer, Julia Dorr. The poem, set in the early 1800s, depicts the hardships suffered by a Rockingham, Vermont, woman who lost her way and wandered for several months in the forests before she stumbled upon a settlement. Dorr claimed her poem was not based on fact. But when Martha drove to Rockingham, she found a descendant of Marjorie Grey who said the poem was an accurate depiction of what had happened. Why would Dorr say she invented the plot? Martha discovered too that the story of Marjorie Grey had been set to music sometime in the nineteenth century by an unknown balladeer and is found in oral circulation in Vermont. Had Dorr really written the poem, or had she based it on a ballad already in existence? Perhaps the descendant of Grey told Martha a bit of family lore that was shaped more by the poem and the ballad than by history. Martha's initial field research raised some important questions about Dorr's sources and about analogues to the poem and about the influence of art on family history. She eventually wrote a textual comparison between the "folk" texts and Dorr's poem, and she outlined the historical and literary contexts of both. A little curiosity, an afternoon trip to Rockingham, and a chance meeting marked the beginning of some original research.

I was asked last spring by a staff member at the university's Robert Hall Fleming Museum to deliver a talk on the relationship between William Carlos Williams and American precisionist painters such as Charles Sheeler and Charles Demuth. Somewhere in my memory, I recalled hearing that there was a link between them, but I had never particularly explored the subject on my own. My research began on three fronts: I went to the museum and viewed the two precisionists works the museum owned. This wasn't enough, so I went to the slide archive in the Art Department. It was a gold mine of slides featuring works by a number of precisionists. My third resource was the library: I checked out several books of precisionist reproductions and a collection of Williams's early poetry. I also located several published studies that deal with exactly what I was researching. I took notes on the art I viewed, on the poetry, and from the critics. No doubt a link existed, but I needed to see that link for myself and to make a case for what I saw. I was, after all, the one delivering the talk, and I was not interested in parroting what others had written.

Starting research may or may not derive from a request or an assignment, but it does come from an honest admission—"I don't know, but I would like to know." Admitting ignorance isn't a problem. Someone once told me that it's impossible to know everything, but everyone ought to know how to find out everything. Remember the student who wanted to write about Fitzgerald and Zelda? The problem was that she already knew what she would write. As a result, her paper suffered from a lack of excitement. In literary scholarship, we probably begin with a curiosity about an author, the text, and/or the reading of a text by an audience. Broad beginnings, admittedly, but a start just the same. Tom wanted to know if Darl was a schizophrenic—a question of how he read the text. Martha began with a historical interest in a poem, but her fieldwork opened up whole new issues worth pursuing. I wanted to see the relationship between paintings (visual texts) and poems (printed texts). We all reached out for help and in return were able to give something back to the community of scholars in the form of our essays or lectures.

The types of research we undertake are limited by our imagination and the amount of time we have to work on a project. I spent about four months on the Williams lecture. I'm not an art historian and had a great deal to learn about the precisionists and about the early poetry of Williams. Tom and Martha each spent about about two weeks researching; Marsha spent a couple of hours. We all used the library. Marsha learned nothing new and contributed nothing new to the scholarly community. Tom, Martha, and I finished our projects a little wiser about our subjects and could take pride in making a scholarly contribution.

□

Field Research and Interviewing

The library, as I mentioned, is probably the resource literary researchers use most often, but it is not necessarily the only or best source of information. Innovative researchers discover their own best resource, and sometimes even generate their body of data. Linda was in an English course that touched on the idea of the affective nature of literature, how texts affect readers. She found herself crying over parts of *Uncle Tom's Cabin,* but wanted to know why she was so moved and whether she was alone in her reaction. She made up a questionnaire and took it along with a particularly emotionally moving passage from the novel to a group of freshmen. They read the passage and then filled out the questionnaire, which asked about how they were affected by the passage. Linda was generating her own data. Based on it, she wrote a very intriguing paper about readers' identification with characters and how this identification affects their sentiments as they read the passage.

Ken Macrorie writes: "The worse place you can begin your search is at the card catalogue in the library. Go to people. They're alive this year, up to date—and the books listed in the file cards aren't" (89). He is speaking about what he calls the "I-search" paper, but with only slight reservation, what he asserts is good advice for the literary research writer.

Unlike library research, the interview gives the researcher the opportunity to question writers and critics about their works, their studies, and their lives. Undergraduates should not ignore the possibility of interviewing local writers and scholars and guest visitors to the campus. College campuses have faculty who are experts in various fields. Tom's interviews with a professor and a social worker provided him with ideas that helped shape his thinking and his writing. Within every English Department there are specialists who are generally more than willing to be interviewed.

Some simple advice expedites a successful interview:

1. Contact interviewees several days in advance. A phone call is all it usually takes. Explain what you are doing and why you wish to interview them. Be specific. Tell them what topic you are researching. If you plan on tape-recording the interview, ask for approval ahead of time.

2. Prepare yourself for the interview. Do a little research and create an extended list of questions. If you plan on interviewing professionals on campus, ask the department secretary for the interviewees' professional vitae and read over the relevant material they published. As a folklorist, I am often interviewed by freshmen for their writing courses. Both of us find the interview frustrating and less than productive when the interviewer is not prepared with a substantial list of well-conceived questions. Two or three questions is nowhere near enough. Remember that an interview is not a conversation, an informal bull session, or a fishing expedition.

Don't expect your experts to lead the interview. You want particular information. Go prepared to conduct the interview confidently. A good list of specific questions can help provide that confidence.

3. If your interviewees are agreeable and you will tape the interview, know your equipment—especially the quirks of microphones—beforehand. Without getting into technical difficulties, I should mention that different mikes function best in special settings. Spend some time learning how well the microphone you will use picks up voices at various distances and with different background noises. Avoid using batteries. They seemed to be programed to fail when needed.

4. Be on time for the interview, and don't forget paper and a pencil. If the recording equipment becomes a distraction or is not functioning properly, put it aside at once and be thankful you brought paper and pencil. In addition, it's always wise to take notes during the interview. You will want to write down unusual terms and the spelling of names and places. At the very beginning, jot down the time, date, and place where the interviewed is conducted, and the names of those present. Then begin asking questions and listening carefully to the answers. Don't interrupt your interviewees, even if they aren't answering your question. Wait until they are done, and rephrase the question. If you talk over their voice the tape will become gibberish; the machine cannot distinguish between voices as well as the human ear. Ask the questions you have prepared, but always be ready to follow another line of questioning if something worth pursuing comes up. Then return to the next question on your list. But remember, no matter how famous or intimidating your interviewees are, you are in charge of the interview. Ask questions forthrightly. Don't hesitate to ask how to spell unusual terms and proper names. If your interviewees start using "they" or "it," make it clear to whom or what "they" or "it" refers. And before you leave, get your interviewees' permission to quote them. Get it in writing, or at least on the tape.

5. Immediately after the interview, sit down with your notes and tape, if you have one, and review the interview. Does what you heard an hour ago still make sense? Do you have the correct spelling of proper names and unusual terms? Once again, check to make sure that the "they's" and "she's" and "there's" and "then's" are clear. If you are missing vital information, call your interviewees and get the information straight. Maybe you might even want to make a follow-up visit just to clarify obscure points.

Attending public readings and lectures is another method of research. Poets sometimes take questions during or after their presentation. Guest scholars present public lectures on campus. Even class lectures are contexts for doing research. Go, listen, and take notes. Ask questions directly related to the topic and get your professor's perspective. If you want to tape a lecture or poetry reading, or any public presentation, always get permission from the speaker and the sponsoring organization beforehand.

And always note the date and place of the interview or lecture. This is information you will need when you document your research in your paper.

□

Using the Library

The library is probably the most obvious resource for literature scholars since the bulk of their research lies with print, either the primary texts themselves or the secondary texts written about them. Learning to use a library efficiently and effectively is one of the most important skills a student of literature, whether an undergraduate or a professor, needs to develop. Fortunately, literary scholarship, like all the fields of human thought, has generated a vast amount of material that may reduce the workload of the experienced researcher.

The library is fundamentally a research facility at the service of a college's students and faculty. The basic tools for initial research include various bibliographies, checklists, indexes, and the card catalogue. Recently, libraries have been installing facilities for computer research. Approaching these resources may seem intimidating, but an hour spent learning where the major research tools are kept will lessen both the footwork and the anxiety.

A couple of very general research tools can point toward specific sources for literary research. For example, if you want to know where to turn to get some information about sources for studies on Alexander Pope or Michael Dorris, a number of guides can help. One is Richard Altick and Andrew Wright's *Selective Bibliography for the Study of English and American Literature* (6th ed. New York: Macmillan, 1969). Although dated, this book lists all journals, reference guides, and bibliographies that you would probably need for your research. Knowing the period or author you wish to work with, you simply consult the *Selective Bibliography* for the names of particular journals and books that deal with the period or author. Another more recent resource is Robert H. Miller's *Handbook of Literary Research* (Metuchen, NJ: Scarecrow Press, 1987). It is a practical guide to the major English and American literature bibliographies.

The *Cambridge Bibliography of English Literature,* edited by F. W. Bateson (4 vols. Cambridge: Cambridge UP, 1940–57) and its successor *The New Cambridge Bibliography of English Literature,* edited by George Watson and Ian Willison (5 vols. Cambridge: Cambridge UP, 1969–77) are important catalogues arranged according to literary periods and genres within those periods. For American authors, consult Jacob Blanck's *Bibliography of American Literature* (New Haven: Yale UP, 1955–) and *American Literary Scholarship: An Annual* (Durham: Duke UP, 1965–).

The most formidable bibliography, simply because of its size and thoroughness, is *The MLA International Bibliography of Books and Articles on the Modern Languages and Literature,* published annually since 1963 by the Modern Language Association. It's the successor to the Association's *Annual Bibliography* (1956–62), which was preceded by *American Bibliography* (1921–53). The *International* is an extremely comprehensive bibliography arranged according to national literatures and subdivided into literary periods. You could, for example, look up American literature, subsection nineteenth century, subsection Henry David Thoreau, and find a list of the many articles published that year regarding Thoreau.

Various scholarly journals specialize in a particular area or genre or national literature and publish appropriate annual bibliographies. For example, from 1917 to 1969, *Studies in Philology (SP)* published annually a bibliography dealing with literature in the Renaissance. From 1926 through 1974, *Philological Quarterly (PQ)* published its annual bibliography for English literature written between 1660 and 1800. Since then, Robert Allen has edited *The Eighteenth Century: A Current Bibliography* (New York: AMS Press, 1979–).

You will discover some esoteric journals and newsletters devoted to a particular author, such as the *Eudora Welty Newsletter,* founded in 1977, and the *Keats-Shelley Journal,* established in 1952. All these resources, as with any bibliography or index, are helpful when the researcher understands how to use them. While you need not master every resource in the library, you should discover what aids are available for the project at hand.

I haven't mention the card catalogue, simply because it is such an obvious source and one you probably already know. Remember that the catalogue is useful for books and manuscripts, but less useful for journals and periodicals. Articles are not identified in a card catalogue, and often journals are more up to date than most books.

Locating resources will go more quickly, the more experience you have. But if you are serious about studying literature, knowing how to locate books and journals and to use bibliographies and card catalogues is an essential part of scholarship. If you have problems, ask a reference librarian. Some libraries offer a user-based computer search service. Learn how to use the equipment before you need to use it.

What about note taking? I'm not going to stress the subject because you have heard about it since grade school. Moreover, every college writing handbook has a section devoted to note taking, explaining how to write down the title, author, publisher, place and date of publication, and page numbers. Similar advice is given for journals and periodicals. It's obvious that if you're planning to cite a source, you need all the publication information in order to make a thorough and accurate statement about exactly where the idea or quote came from. Some people write down such material on index cards; those who use the photocopier write the source information on the back of the copies. If you are using an archive with its own catalogue system, note how one could find the artifact or manuscript you have viewed. The secret is to get all the information down before you begin reading the text, so that if you do use ideas or words from it, you will have all the information at your fingertips.

Failure to offer readers complete and accurate information about sources undermines your own paper and measurably weakens its power to inform or argue. Everything about research writing—your ideas and the ideas from your sources—should be able to withstand serious scrutiny. Research-based papers with weak or inadequate documentation fail to live up to the expectations of a critical audience. Even if you don't use a source directly, you might still want to list it as a work you know about and consulted. Inadequate note taking becomes particularly frustrating when after you have written the body of the paper and are about to write in the citations or create the list of works consulted, your notes are incomplete. What should be a very simple task if adequate notes were taken in the beginning turns into a mad scramble back in the library.

□

Evaluating Sources

While you are collecting information, be it from printed or oral sources, be sure to check it over. If a source is simply wrong or silly, you certainly don't want to use it in your paper. If the notion is outdated and no longer considered a valid point, you don't want to build a paper around it. Ideas do change; what were once considered facts have been disproved by later findings, and critical theories and biases pass in and out of vogue. As Jim Holstun mentions in his chapter, New Criticism was once the rage in literary circles; structuralist criticism has already become passé, and deconstructuralism is on its way out. The books and articles you read are biased according to the school of thought to which their authors subscribe, so you need to evaluate your sources before using them. Of course you may not be able to check every statement and every thesis, but you should try to check sources in a general way.

I've come up with a list of questions which you might ask.

Is the author an authority in the field? Authorities publish more than one or two articles in a specific field. As you look through a bibliography, the names of experts will recur with some frequency. You might also check an author's credentials in reference books such as *Who's Who in America,* the *Directory of American Scholars,* and *Contemporary Authors.* Book reviews evaluate quality. *Book Review Digest* surveys reviews, but one is less apt to find scholarly books with a limited audience appeal reviewed here. For these books, it is necessary to look in the review sections of publications such as *The New York Review of Books* and the London *Times Literary Supplement.* Most major journals also publish reviews of books which relate to their particular specialty. Don't forget to ask classmates or instructors whether they are familiar with the writer or the book or the article.

If none of this proves useful, evaluate the text yourself. How adequate is the documentation? Does it rely chiefly on primary or secondary sources? Is the language vague and loaded with jargon, or specific and concrete? Is the article or book convincing and logical, or does it conflict with common sense or what you have read elsewhere?

How reputable is the publication? Different journal and book publishers may have particular editorial biases, and some publications have a much better reputation as outlets for scholarship than others. Vanity presses—publishing houses an author pays in order to have a text published—are less critical of what they publish than standard publishing houses, which put up the money themselves. Most established journals earn a reputation for their quality publications. Those with editorial review boards that evaluate a submission before publishing it maintain editorial standards and biases. Journals are evaluated for their biases in *Magazines for Libraries* and *Classified List of Periodicals for the College Library*.

Is the scholarship up to date? Scholarship is a cumulative process, with researchers constantly sharing new insights and fresh angles to various topics. Always check the date of publication carefully and then see if the subject has been superseded by more recent publications. Remember too, that journal articles tend to be more up to date than books, simply because book production takes a longer time.

□

Documentation

With your research finished, you are ready to begin writing the paper. I'm not going to review the writing and revising of a paper, but I want to comment on documenting sources. There are two basic questions: What should be documented in a paper? How can quotes be incorporated into a text?

In regard to the first question, Walter S. Achtert and Joseph Gibaldi, authors of *The MLA Style Manual,* write:

> In scholarly writing, everything derived from an outside source requires documentation—not only direct quotations and paraphrases but also information and ideas. Of course, good judgment as well as ethics should guide you in interpreting this rule. Although you rarely need, for example, to give sources for familiar proverbs . . . , well known quotations . . . , or common knowledge . . . , you must indicate the origin of any appropriated material that readers might otherwise mistake for your own. (163)

"Good judgment," "ethics," and "appropriated material" are key phrases. Tom appropriated into his paper ideas from his interviews with the social worker and his psychology professor. He gave them credit in his paper for two reasons: what he quoted were their ideas, and he didn't want to take responsibility for the ideas if they were wrong. There is no justification for authors/researchers/scholars to misrepresent the source of an idea that is not their own; it is simply a matter of professional ethics.

This spring Mark, a junior majoring in English, wrote a brief paper on "The Hippopotamus" by T. S. Eliot. It's a short poem, nine quatrains long. There is, of course, a Latin quotation from St. Ignatius's letter to the Traillians, but the rest is Eliot's poem. As Mark read it, he realized that Eliot compares the "True Church" to the lazy, gluttonous hippo. Mark found the sarcasm particularly interesting, but he was aware that Eliot was not the first to attack abuses within the Catholic Church. The lines "While the True Church can never fail / For it is based upon the rock," Mark felt, particularly emphasize the Church's smugness, and he writes:

> Eliot writes these lines with absolute sarcasm to em-
> phasize the whole theme of the poem—that the Church has
> indeed failed and is lacking in some of the basic ideals
> of Christianity as Christ taught it. This challenge to
> the Church is not new to Eliot, however, as we have seen
> other writings such as Goliardic literature of the Mid-
> dle Ages which were songs and poems in praise of love and
> wine. These were written in direct rebellion against
> the Church because the writers felt that the Church had
> become too wealthy and pompous (Jesus was never rich or
> pompous). When papal power had reached a peak under In-
> nocent III in the late 12the century, new movements of
> criticism were aimed at the Church by such groups as the
> Waldensians and Albigensians. They made many of the
> same claims against the Church as Eliot did in "The Hip-
> popotamus." What makes "The Hippopotamus" a great poem
> is not that it presents a new theme, but that it presents
> an old theme in a new way. (3)

Mark presented information he had learned in a medieval history course, and he didn't need to cite a source for it because the material was truly part of his own knowledge and expressed in his own words. For someone who gathered this information about the medieval Church, a source would have to be cited.

Citations

Before providing some examples of ways of incorporating source material into an essay, I want to present some of the rationale behind documentation procedures. A quotation is the reproduction of the words of another voice in your paper. It may come from an interview or from print. It might be the words of a TV advertisement or a recorded song. In any case, they are not your words and should not be presented as such in your paper.

It is stylistically preferable to cite author's name and source right in the text. The former may be repeated throughout the text whenever necessary, but there is no need to give the title every time you quote the source, if by omitting it there is no confusion. Following each quotation, put a page reference. That is what the "(3)" at the end of my quotation from Mark's paper is. If you are using more than one source by the same author, include in the parentheses shortened titles along with the page number(s).

For the sake of example, I will use the same passage from *Semiotics and Interpretation,* a book by Robert Scholes. What Scholes writes may be heady, but I chose to use it in order to emphasize citation forms, rather than content.

The first examples indicate that I have taken Scholes's idea and put it into my own words, a kind of paraphrase.

```
Robert Scholes in his study Semiotics and Interpreta-
tion does not see the semiotic approach to literature as
radically different from other approaches, but as a
critical method which considers the text from a differ-
ent perspective and draws upon a methodology born out of
the study of semiotics. (110)
```

The advantage of the paraphrase is that I can condense my sources' ideas and use only the essential ideas. After all, the purpose of using sources in the first place is usually for the ideas in them and not necessarily their words, unless the words are themselves significant.

Sometimes, however, I may want to use the words of a source. I can incorporate them into my own sentence.

```
In his study Semiotics and Literature, Robert Scholes
states that a semiotic approach to a literary text "is
not wholly unlike a traditional interpretation or rhe-
torical analysis, nor it is meant to replace these other
modes of response to literary works." (110)
```

If the quotation is less than four typed lines (about thirty-five to forty words), incorporate it directly into your own text as I have done above. If the quotation is longer than four typed lines, indent the quotation ten spaces from the left margin.

```
Robert Scholes, in his critical study Semiotics and
Literature, does not view the semiotic approach to a
```

literary text as a radical departure from more traditional approaches to literary studies, but he does recognize some differences between them:

> Most interpretive methods privilege the "meaning"
> of the text. Hermeneutic critics seek authorial or
> intentional meaning; the New Critics seek the am-
> biguities of "textual" meaning; the "reader re-
> sponse" critics allow readers to make meaning. With
> respect to meaning the semiotic critic is situated
> differently. Such a critic looks for the generic or
> discursive structures that enable and constrain
> meaning. (110)

When quoting a statement of another, quote only what is relevant.
Quote directly only when the words of your source are strikingly important, or you are unable to present the idea in any better way; otherwise,
paraphrase the idea in your own words.

Had I not cited Scholes's name, I would include it in the parentheses,
preceding the page number and not separated from it by a comma:
"(Scholes 110)." If I am using other sources also written by Scholes, I make
clear in my text or in my citation which source I am citing: "(Scholes
Semiotics 110)."

Poetry is quoted differently because of its form. Like a prose quote, try
to weave the author and title into your text, at least the first time you quote
from a particular poem. One line of poetry is simply written in quotation
marks without any indentation:

> Shelley begins his elegiac poem "Adonais" with a force
> unmatched in literature: "I weep for Adonais—he is
> dead!" (line 1).

Two or three lines are written into your text with a "space-slash-space"
separating the verses:

> Shelley' elegiac poem "Adonais" begins with the poet
> expressing his intense grief for the fallen god: "I weep
> for Adonais—he is dead! / Oh, weep for Adonais! though
> our tear / Thaw not the frost which binds so dear a head!"
> (lines 1-3)

For more than three lines, indent ten lines from the left and begin each
verse on a new line:

> In "Adonais," Shelley expressed his grief for the
> fallen god and invites all to weep for him:

I weep for Adonais—he is dead!
Oh, weep for Adonais! though our tears
Thaw not the frost which binds so dear a head!
And thou, sad Hour, selected from all years
To mourn our loss, rouse thy obscure compeers,
And teach them thine own sorrow! (lines 1–6)

What about interviews? material from phonograph records? photographs? survey results? Weave into your text pertinent source material as much as possible:

```
When I interviewed Professor O'Bryan he stated: "Shel-
ley began "Adonais" following the elegiac formula es-
tablished in classical literary tradition."
```

Remember, the purpose of the citations in the text is to make a quick source identification, but the reader may refer to the list of sources cited at the end of the paper for more complete reference information. Fuzzy citations weaken the plausibility of a research paper, and suggest that the authors do not have control over their research or their information.

Is there a limit to the number of quotations a research paper should have? The answer is no, but common sense and stylistic concerns should be taken into account. A page of typed text that has ten citations looks rather silly, unless there is a particular point in terms of the sources themselves which the writer of the paper is trying to make. But there is no hard and fast rule: Just don't detract from your paper by making it look silly with too many references crowded together.

Footnotes

Footnotes have not vanished from scholarly writing, although writers tend to replace them with endnotes, not to be confused with lists of works cited or consulted. For years, all citations were put in footnotes at the bottom of a page or in endnotes placed after the text but before the bibliography. With the shortened internal forms I have described becoming more widely used, notes—foot or end—are limited more often to what is called informational or content notes. If you need to explain something about your text—perhaps you used an unusual research method that needs some explaining or you want readers to be aware of a particular idea or problem—but don't feel that the information properly belongs in the text itself, use a content note. Place a superscript number in the text where you think the reader needs to have the explanation and put that information at the bottom of the page or at the end of the text, identifying it with the same superscript number. Perhaps you wish to describe some field research procedures you used in your paper. Your text reads:

> Besides exploring my own responses to *Uncle Tom's Cabin*, I sought information about how others respond.[1]

Your footnote or endnote reads:

> [1]On April 30, 1987, I distributed 75 questionnaires to students enrolled in English 3, sections 3, 7, and 12. A copy of the questionnaire is in Appendix One. Appendix Two details all of the responses to the questionnaire. I also gave each student a copy of "The Slave Warehouse" chapter of *Uncle Tom's Cabin*, and their responses to the questionnaire dealt with their reading of that chapter.

Most writers avoid using these notes at all, reasoning that if the information is important enough, they will work it into the text.

Works Cited

Once the main part of the paper is written, you need to create a list showing where your sources may be found. You have given an author, title, and page number, but that isn't enough information. Your reader may want to know dates, editions, volume numbers, and so forth.

The term "Bibliography" is no longer used in research circles; it has been replaced by "Works Cited" and "Works Consulted." The difference between the latter two is simple: the former lists only the sources you actually paraphrased, quoted from, or took ideas from; "Works Consulted" lists sources that may have influenced your thinking, but in a less specific way. You found these helpful, and although you did not particularly rely upon them, you want readers to know you consulted them. Most of my students are content with only a list of works cited, but most critical readers, including teachers, want to see how thorough the research was and like to see "Works Consulted."

Here are examples of various types of citations. I have not tried to be exhaustive, but to present those my students most commonly need to follow. For a more complete set of examples, English students should refer to *The MLA Style Manual* or to the forms prescribed by the class instructor.

NONWRITTEN SOURCES

INTERVIEW

Feldman, Henry. Personal interview. 29 June 1988.

PHONOGRAPH RECORDING

MacArthur, Margaret. "When the Wind's in the West." *An Almanac of New England Farm Songs.* Green Linnet, SIF 1039, 1982.

ART WORKS (if you are using the original, otherwise treat reproduction in book like an essay from a collection)

Lachaise, Gaston. "The Mountain." Metropolitan Museum of Art, Alfred Stieglitz Collection.

WRITTEN SOURCES

BOOKS

Basic format

Scholes, Robert. *Semiotics and Interpretation.* New Haven: Yale UP, 1982.

Two or three authors

Barzum, Jacques, and Henry F. Graff. *The Modern Researcher.* Rev. ed. New York: Harcourt, Brace & World, 1970.

Republished texts

Twain, Mark. *Adventures of Huckleberry Finn.* 1885. Berkeley: University of California Press, 1985.

Essay reprinted in a collection

Lewis, C. S. "What Chaucer Really Did to *Il Filostrato.*" *Essays and Studies by Members of the English Association* 17 (1932): 56–75. Rpt. in *Troilus and Criseyde & The Minor Poems.* Vol. 2 of *Chaucer Criticism.* Eds. Richard J. Schoech and Jerome Taylor. South Bend: University of Notre Dame Press, 1961. 16–33.

JOURNALS AND PERIODICALS

BASIC FORM FOR SCHOLARLY JOURNAL

Clements, William M. "The Ethnic Joke as a Mirror of Culture." *New York Folklore Quarterly* 12.3–4 (1986): 87–97.

NEWSPAPER

Shaw, Kent. " 'Amazing' Daisy Turner Nearly 104." *Burlington Free Press* 3 June 1987, 1A+.

POPULAR JOURNAL

Robison, Mary. "Seizing Control." *The New Yorker* 25 May 1987: 35–36.

All this concern over correct citations and lists of works consulted is not particularly formidable. With practice, most of it becomes automatic. But researchers usually keep *The MLA Style Manual* handy, and every college library has at least one copy. Research projects ought not to become bogged down in prescriptions; they are simply means by which a student of literature can pursue scholarly interests. Learning how to undertake and to use research in one's writing and for intellectual growth is part of becoming a professional in the field.

☐

Works Cited

Achtert, Walter S., and Joseph Gibaldi. *The MLA Style Manual.* New York: Modern Language Association, 1985.

Macrorie, Ken. *Searching Writing.* Upper Montclair, NJ: Boynton/Cook, 1984.

McNiff, Mark. Manuscript of "Eliot and the Church." Department of English, University of Vermont [Spring 1987].

Shelley, Percy Bysshe. "Adonais." Rpt. in *How Does a Poem Mean?* Eds. John Ciardi and Miller Williams. 2nd ed. Boston: Houghton Mifflin, 1975. 176–87.

Scholes, Robert. *Semiotics and Interpretation.* New Haven: Yale UP, 1982.

Glossary

Action A series of events that moves the work from one point to the next.

Alliteration The repetition of initial consonant sounds, as "On the bald street breaks the blank day."

Antagonist A character or force which opposes the main character, or **protagonist**, in a plot.

Atmosphere A mood or emotional aura.

Audience Those to whom writing is directed.

Characters The people in fictional narratives.

Climax (a) A moment of emotional or intellectual intensity; (b) a point in the plot at which one opposing force overcomes another and the conflict is resolved.

Conflict A struggle between opposing forces or characters.

Connotation What a word suggests, beyond its dictionary meaning.

Conventions The familiar structures which literary texts use to create meaning, as the dramatic aside or the Shakespearean soliloquy.

Denotation The dictionary definition of what a word means.

Diction The choice of particular words whose educational, social, and situational levels help create meaning.

Documentation The form by which one gives credit for materials taken from other sources.

Epiphany A flash of intuitive understanding.

Figurative language Language which deviates from the literal in order to suggest special meanings or effects. Metaphors and similes are examples of figurative language.

Focalization The use of a character's perspective to tell part, or all, of a story.

Genre A literary form, such as poetry, fiction, drama, autobiography, or essay.

Imagery Language which appeals directly to one of the five senses.

Literary criticism The practice of posing and answering interpretive questions about literary texts.

Literary theory The practice of posing and answering interpretive questions about competing critical forms.

Lyric A fairly short, concentrated, and song-like poem (originally sung to a lyre).

Metadrama A drama which calls attention to its form as a drama, as when a drama has, as part of its setting, a poster for the play which is being performed.

Metaphor A comparison between two things; a direct comparison as opposed to the indirect comparison of the **simile**. "He is a lion in the field" is a metaphor.

Narrator Someone who tells a story. A **character narrator** tells a story in which he or she is involved; an **omniscient narrator** tells a story about other people.

Parody Writing which imitates the style, form, or theme of another work.

Pathos The evocation of the feelings of tenderness, pity, or sympathetic sorrow.

Persona A self invented by the author to present a poem, story, essay, or other piece of writing.

Plagiarism Deliberately presenting the words or ideas of another writer as if they were one's own.

Plot The events which happen and why they happen.

Poetics The study of the codes and conventions which give literary texts meaning.

Point of view (a) the narrative vantage point from which a literary work is told; (b) the position from which one sees a drama.

Protagonist The main character, or "hero/heroine", of a plot.

Rhyme The repetition of sounds, usually at the ends of lines of poems, but often recurring at regular places in the line, as moon, June, and spittoon.

Rhythm The rise and fall of stress, within single words or in larger units such as sentences, paragraphs, speeches, and poems, as in "With a leap and a bound the swift Anapests throng."

Setting The general locale in which the action occurs.

Simile An indirect comparison which uses the words "like" or "as"; distinguished from **metaphor.** "He is like a lion in the field" is a simile.

Style The particular way in which a writer uses words, including diction, sentence length, degree of formality and complexity, etc.

Symbol An object which represents itself and, through association, something else of an abstract nature, such as the white whale in *Moby Dick.*

Theme The meaning or meanings embodied in a work of literature.

Thesis The essential argument of a piece of nonfiction writing, such as a critical paper.

Tone The attitude toward self, subject, and audience contained in a piece of writing.

Transitions Words, scenes, or actions which show the relationship between the preceding and the ensuing sections of a work.

Voice An individual style or point of view through which a writer may be identified.

Biographies of the Contributors

The contributors are colleagues in the English department at the University of Vermont.

ARTHUR W. BIDDLE teaches American literature and writing. He is editor of the *Writer's Guide* series and co-author of *Writer's Guide: Life Sciences* and *Writer's Guide: Political Science.* He is currently writing a play about Thomas Merton, Trappist monk.

MARY JANE DICKERSON teaches composition and literature. She is co-author of two books on writing, *Until I See What I Say* and *Writer's Guide: History,* and author of essays on several American writers. Currently she is exploring forms of autobiography and the personal essay about literature.

TOBY FULWILER teaches writing and American literature. He is author and editor of several books including *Language Connections* (1982), *Teaching with Writing* (1987), and *The Journal Book* (1987), as well as numerous articles on writing across the curriculum.

JAMES HOLSTUN teaches Renaissance English literature and literary theory. He has published on Shakespeare's *Coriolanus* and on lesbianism in Renaissance English poetry, and is the author of *A Rational Millennium,* a study of Puritan utopian writing. He is now at work on a study of the rhetoric of radical sectarians during the English Revolution.

JAMES HOWE has been modifying his writing classes for three decades, and his Shakespeare classes for two. Author of books on writing and on Christopher Marlowe, he is presently at work on a study of Shakespeare's plays in their historical, artistic and religious contexts.

TONY MAGISTRALE teaches courses in American literature and directs the freshman composition program. He is the author of *Writer's Guide: Psychology* and *Landscape of Fear: Stephen King's American Gothic.*

SIDNEY POGER teaches a variety of courses including Detective Fiction, Modern Poetry, and genre studies. He has published essays on numerous poets, from his first piece on William Cullen Bryant to his latest on W.H. Auden.

ALLEN SHEPHERD teaches American literature and creative writing. He has published fiction, poetry, prose translations, and personal, critical and scholarly essays in American, Canadian, and European periodicals.

WILLIAM A. STEPHANY teaches a variety of courses on medieval literature and culture. He has published several essays on medieval literature and is co-author of a forthcoming book on Dante's *Inferno.*

RICHARD SWETERLITSCH teaches courses in folklore, composition, and American literature. He has published in the *Folklore Forum* and *Journal of American Folklore* and has edited *The Oral History Review.* He is managing editor of *Proverbium* and is currently completing a study of a legend complex surrounding the Lake Champlain monster.

ROBYN R. WARHOL specializes in feminist theory, narratology, and nineteenth-century fiction. She has published essays on George Eliot, Elizabeth Gaskell, and Harriet Beecher Stowe. Currently she is revising a book manuscript on gender and narrative interventions.

Index

Bold face indicates that the term is defined in the Glossary.

Index